THE
AUTHENTICITY
OF THE
BIBLE

Original Title:
The Bible and Its Christ

THE
AUTHENTICITY
OF THE
BIBLE

ASSURANCE THAT THE
BIBLE IS THE WORD OF GOD

REUBEN A. TORREY

We love hearing from our readers. Please contact us at www.anekopress.com/questions-comments with any questions, comments, or suggestions.

Contents

Chapter 1

Why I Believe That the Bible Is the Word of God

Is the Bible the Word of God? That is the most important question in religious thought. If the Bible is the Word of God, if it is an absolutely trustworthy revelation from God Himself of Himself, His purposes and His will, of man's duty and destiny, and of spiritual and eternal realities, then we have a starting point from which we can proceed to the conquest of the whole domain of religious truth.

However, if the Bible is not the Word of God, if it is the mere product of man's thinking, speculation, and guessing, if it is not altogether trustworthy in regard to religious and eternal truth, then we are all at sea, not knowing where we are drifting, but we can be sure that we are not drifting toward any safe port.

I did not always believe that the Bible is the Word of God. I sincerely doubted that the Bible was the Word of

God. I doubted that Jesus Christ was the Son of God. I doubted whether there was a personal God. I was not an infidel, but I was a skeptic. I did not deny it, but I questioned it. I was not an atheist, but I was an agnostic. I did not know, but I was determined to find out.

If there was a God, I was determined to find that out and act accordingly. If there was not a God, I was determined to find that out and act accordingly. If Jesus Christ was the Son of God, I was determined to find that out and act accordingly. If Jesus Christ was not the Son of God, I was determined to find that out and act accordingly. If the Bible was the Word of God, I was determined to find that out and act accordingly. If the Bible was not the Word of God, I was determined to find that out and act accordingly.

Well, I found out. I found out beyond a doubt that there is a God, that Jesus Christ is the Son of God, and that the Bible is the Word of God. Today it is not just a matter of mere probability with me, nor even of mere belief, but it is a matter of absolute certainty.

I am now going to give you some of the reasons why I believe that the Bible is the Word of God. I will not give you all the reasons, for it would take months to do that. I will not even give you the reasons that are most convincing to me personally, for these are based upon my experience and are often so personal that they cannot be appropriately explained to another.

However, I will give you reasons that will prove conclusive to anyone who is honestly and unbiasedly seeking the truth and who desires to know the truth and is willing to obey it. These reasons will not convince anyone who is determined not to know the truth or who is unwilling to obey it. If someone will not receive the love of the truth, he must be left to his own deliberate choice of error, given over to strong delusion to believe a lie (2 Thessalonians 2:11). However, if someone is searching for the truth, no matter how completely uncertain or confused he might be, he can be led into the truth.

Reason 1: The Testimony of Jesus Christ

I believe the Bible is the Word of God because of the testimony of Jesus Christ to that fact. We live in a day in which many people say that they accept the teaching of Jesus Christ, but that they do not accept the teaching of the whole Bible. They say that they believe what Jesus Christ says, but they are not sure if they believe what Moses said, or is said to have said, or what Isaiah said, or is said to have said, or what Jeremiah said, or Paul said, or John said, or that they are not sure about the rest of the Bible writers.

This position may at first seem rational, but in reality it is completely irrational. If we accept the teaching of Jesus Christ, we must accept the whole Bible, for Jesus Christ has set the stamp of His authority upon the entire Book. If we accept His authority, we must accept all that He sets the stamp of His authority upon.

Old Testament
As to Christ's endorsement of the Old Testament, look first at Mark 7:13. Jesus had just quoted from

the law of Moses. He did not just quote from the Ten Commandments, but He also quoted from other portions of the law of Moses. He set the teaching of the law of Moses against the traditions of the Pharisees and scribes. In this verse, He said, *You make the word of God of none effect through your tradition.* He distinctly called the law of Moses *the word of God.*

It is sometimes said that the Bible nowhere claims to be the Word of God, yet here Jesus Christ Himself distinctly asserted that the law of Moses is the Word of God. If, then, we accept the authority of Jesus Christ, we must accept the law of Moses as the Word of God. Of course, this only covers the first five books of the Old Testament, but if we can accept this as the Word of God, we will have little difficulty with the rest of the Old Testament, for it is here that the hottest battle is being fought today.

Now turn to Matthew 5:18. Here Jesus says, *Till heaven and earth pass away, one jot or one tittle shall in nowise pass from the law until all be fulfilled.* Every Hebrew scholar knows that a "jot" is the Hebrew character "yodh," the smallest character in the Hebrew alphabet, less than half the size of any other character in the Hebrew alphabet. A "tittle" is a little horn that the Hebrews put on their consonants. Jesus here asserts that the law of Moses as originally given is absolutely infallible down to its smallest letter and part of a letter. If, then, we accept the authority of Jesus Christ, we must accept the authority of the law of Moses as originally given and as contained in the Old Testament Scriptures.

Look next at John 10:35. Jesus had just quoted from

one of the Psalms to prove a point He was making, and then He added, *The Scripture cannot be broken*, thus setting the stamp of His authority upon the absolute reliability and irrefutability of the Old Testament Scriptures.

Turn now to Luke 24:27, and you will read that Jesus, *beginning at Moses and all the prophets, expounded unto them in all the Scriptures the things concerning Himself.* In verse 44 of that same chapter, He says, *All things must be fulfilled which were written in the law of Moses, and in the prophets, and in the Psalms.* Every scholar knows that the Jews divided their Bible (our present Old Testament Scriptures) into three parts: the Law (the first five books of the Old Testament), the Prophets (most of the books that we call prophetic, and some of those that we call historical), and the Psalms or Sacred Writings, which are the remaining books of the Old Testament. Jesus Christ takes up each one of these three recognized divisions of the Old Testament Scriptures and sets the stamp of His authority upon each of them. If, then, we accept the authority of Jesus Christ, we are driven logically to accept the entire Old Testament Scriptures.

> If, then, we accept the authority of Jesus Christ, we are driven logically to accept the entire Old Testament Scriptures.

In Luke 16:31, Jesus says, *If they hear not Moses and the prophets, neither will they be persuaded though one be raised from the dead.* Thus, in the most emphatic way, He endorsed the truth of the Old Testament Scriptures.

In John 5:47, He says, *If ye believe not his [Moses']*

writings, how shall ye believe My words? Here He sets the stamp of His authority upon the teaching of Moses as being just as truly from God as His own was. If, then, we accept the authority of Jesus Christ, we must accept the entire Old Testament.

New Testament

What about the New Testament? Did Jesus set His stamp of authority upon it also? He did. How could He have done so, though, when not a book of the New Testament was written when He departed from this earth? He did so by way of anticipation. Turn to John 14:26 and you will hear Jesus saying, *The Comforter, which is the Holy Ghost, whom the Father will send in My name, He shall teach you all things and bring all things to your remembrance whatsoever I have said unto you.* He therefore set the stamp of His authority not just upon the apostolic teaching as given by the Holy Spirit, but upon the apostolic recollection of what He Himself had taught.

The question is often asked, "How do we know that we have an accurate account of the teaching of Jesus Christ in the Gospels?" It is asked, "Did the apostles take notes at the time of what Jesus said?" There is reason to believe that they did, that Matthew and Peter, from whom Mark derived his material, and James (from whom, there is reason to believe, Luke obtained much of his material) took notes of what Jesus said in Aramaic, and that John took notes of what Jesus said in Greek, and that we have in the four Gospels the report of what they wrote down at the time.

But whether this is true or not does not matter for

our present purposes, for we have Christ's own authority for it that in the apostolic records we do not merely have the apostles' remembrance of what Jesus said, but we have the Holy Spirit's remembrance of what Jesus said. While the apostles might forget and report inaccurately, the Holy Spirit could not forget.

Turn to John 16:12-13, and you will hear Jesus saying, *I have yet many things to say unto you, but ye cannot bear them now. Howbeit when He, the Spirit of truth, is come, He will guide you into all truth.* Here Jesus sets the stamp of His authority upon the teaching of the apostles as being given by the Holy Spirit, as containing all the truth, and as containing more truth than His own teaching. He tells the apostles that He has many things that He knows to tell them, but that they are not ready yet to receive them. However, Jesus tells them that when the Holy Spirit comes, He will guide them into this fuller and larger truth.

If, then, we accept the authority of Jesus Christ, we must accept the apostolic teaching, the New Testament writings, as being given through the Holy Spirit, as containing all the truth, and as containing more truth than Jesus taught while on earth. There are many in our day who are crying out, "Back to Christ," by which they usually mean, "We do not care what Paul taught, or what John taught, or what James taught, or what Jude taught. We do not know about them. Let us go back to Christ, the original source of authority, and accept what He taught, and that alone."

Very well. "Back to Christ." The cry is not a bad one, but when you get back to Christ, you hear Christ

Himself saying, "On to the apostles. They have more truth to teach than I have taught. The Holy Spirit has taught them all the truth. Listen to them." If, then, we accept the authority of Jesus Christ, we are driven to accept the authority of the entire New Testament.

Therefore, if we accept the teaching of Jesus Christ, we must accept the entire Old Testament and the entire New Testament. It is either Christ and the whole Bible, or no Bible and no Christ.

There are some in these days who say that they believe in Christ, but not in the Christ of the New Testament. But there is no Christ except the Christ of the New Testament. Any other Christ than the Christ of the New Testament is a pure figment of the imagination. Any other Christ than the Christ of the New Testament is an idol made by man's own ideas, and whoever worships him is an idolater.

Five Divine Testimonies

We must accept the authority of Jesus Christ. He is accredited to us by five unmistakable divine testimonies.

First, He is accredited to us by the testimony of the divine life that He lived, for He lived as no other man lived. Let anyone take the four Gospels for himself and read them carefully and candidly, and he will soon be convinced of two things.

He will first see that he is reading the story of a life actually lived. No one could have made up the character set forth in the Gospels unless the life had been actually lived. Much less could four men have made up such a person, each one of the four making his own account of that character that is not only consistent with itself, but is consistent with the other three. To suppose that these four men who wrote the Gospels dreamed up the life of Jesus would be to suppose a greater miracle than any recorded in the Gospels.

He will see, in the second place, that the life set forth in the Gospels is apart from all other human lives. It stands by itself and is clearly a divine life lived under human conditions. Napoleon Bonaparte was a good

> No one could have made up the character set forth in the Gospels unless the life had been actually lived.

judge of men. He once said regarding the life of Jesus as recorded in the Gospels, which he had been reading, "I know men [and if he did not know men, whoever did?], and Jesus Christ was not a man." What he meant was, of course, that Jesus Christ was not a mere man.

Second, Jesus Christ is accredited to us by the divine words that He spoke. If anyone will study the teaching of Jesus Christ with honesty and faithfulness, he will soon see that it has a character that distinguishes it from all other teaching ever uttered on earth.

Third, Jesus Christ was accredited to us by the divine works that He did, not only healing the sick, which many others have done, but cleansing the leper, opening the eyes of the blind, raising the dead, calming the storm by a word, turning water into wine, and feeding five thousand men with five small loaves and two small fish, which was a creative act. These miracles of power are clear credentials of a God-sent teacher. We cannot study them honestly and not come to the same conclusion as Nicodemus: *We know that You are a teacher come from God, for no man can do these signs that You do, except God be with him* (John 3:2).

Of course, we bear in mind the fact that strenuous efforts have been made to eliminate the supernatural element from the story of the life of Jesus Christ, but all these efforts have resulted in failure, and all similar efforts will result in failure. The most able effort of this kind that was ever made was that of David Strauss in his *Leben Jesu*, or *Life of Jesus*.

David Strauss was a man of remarkable ability and gifts, a man of real and profound scholarship, a man of notable genius, a man with remarkable power of critical analysis, and a man of steadfast perseverance and untiring activity. He focused all the rare gifts of his richly endowed mind upon the story of the life of Jesus with the determination to discredit the miraculous element contained therein. He spent his best years and strength in this effort.

If anyone could have succeeded in such an effort, David Strauss was the man, but he failed utterly. For a little while, it seemed to many that he had succeeded in his purpose, but when his life of Jesus was itself submitted to rigid, critical analysis, it fell all to pieces, and today is utterly discredited.

Those who want to eliminate the miraculous element in the story of Jesus feel that they must make the attempt anew since the attempt of David Strauss has come to nothing. Where David Strauss failed, Ernest Renan tried again. He did not have, by any means, the ability and genius of Strauss, but he was a man of brilliant genius, of subtle imagination, of rare literary skill, and of extraordinary skill and ability.

Renan's *Life of Christ* was read with interest and admiration by many. The work was done with fascinating skill. Some imagined that Ernest Renan had succeeded in his attempt, but his *Life of Jesus* naturally enough was discredited even in a shorter time than that of David Strauss. All other attempts have met with a similar fate. It is an attempt at the impossible.

Let any honest person take the life of Jesus and read it for himself with attention and care, and he will soon discover that the life described there could not have been imagined, but must have been really lived, that the teachings reported as uttered by Jesus are not fictitious teachings put into the mouth of a fictitious person, but are the real utterances of a real person.

He will also discover that the character and the teaching set forth in the Gospels are inseparably interwoven with the stories of the miracles. He will find that if you eliminate the miracles, the character and the teaching disappear, for the character and teachings cannot be separated from the miraculous element without a brutality of treatment that no reasonable person will allow.

At least this much is proven today, that Jesus lived and worked mainly as is recorded in the four Gospels. Personally, I believe that more than this is proven, but this is enough for our present purpose. If Jesus lived and worked basically as the Gospels record, cleansing the lepers, opening the eyes of the blind, raising the dead, calming the storm with His word, and feeding the five thousand with five small loaves and two small fish, then He bears unmistakable credentials as a teacher sent and endorsed by God.

Fourth, Jesus Christ is also accredited to us by His divine influence upon all subsequent history. Jesus Christ was beyond doubt one of three things: (1) He was either the Son of God in a unique sense, a divine Person incarnate in human form, (2) He was the most daring impostor who ever lived, or else (3) He was one of the most hopeless lunatics who ever lived.

There can be no honest doubt that He claimed to be the Son of God in a unique sense, that He said that all people should honor Him even as they honored the Father (John 5:23), that He said that He and the Father were one (John 10:30), and that He taught that those who had seen Him had seen the Father (John 14:9). He was then either the divine Person who He claimed to be, He was the most daring impostor ever, or He was a most hopeless lunatic.

Was His influence upon subsequent history the influence of a lunatic? No one but a lunatic would say so. Was His influence upon subsequent history the influence of an impostor? Only someone whose own heart was thoroughly corrupted with deceit and fraud would think of saying so. Not being an impostor or a lunatic, then, we have only one alternative left: He was who He claimed to be – the Son of God.

Fifth, Jesus Christ is accredited to us by His resurrection from the dead. I will later present to you the evidence for the resurrection of Jesus Christ. We will see that the historic evidence for the resurrection of Christ is absolutely convincing in its character. The resurrection of Jesus Christ from the dead is one of the best proven facts of history, but the resurrection of Christ is God's seal to Christ's claim.

Jesus Christ claimed to be the Son of God. He was put to death for making that claim. Before being put to death, He said that God would set His seal to the claim by raising Him from the dead. They killed Him. They laid Him in the sepulcher. They rolled a stone to the door of the sepulcher. They sealed that door with the Roman seal, and it meant death to anyone who broke that seal.

When the appointed hour came, of which Christ had spoken, the breath of God swept through the sleeping clay and Jesus rose triumphant over death. God spoke more clearly than if He would speak from the open heavens today and say, *This is My beloved Son: Hear Him* (Luke 9:35).

If we are honest, then, we must accept the authority of Jesus Christ. As already seen, if we accept the authority of Jesus Christ, we must accept the entire Old Testament and the entire New Testament as being the Word of God. Therefore, I believe that the Bible is the Word of God because of the testimony of Jesus Christ to that effect.

A school of criticism has arisen that is trying to gain credibility by opposing the authority of Jesus Christ.

They say, for example, "Jesus said that the eleventh psalm was by David and was messianic, but we say that the eleventh psalm is not by David and is not messianic." They ask us to give up the authority and infallibility of Jesus Christ and the Bible, wanting us to accept their authority and their infallibility in their place.

Very well, but before doing so, we demand their credentials. We do not yield to the claim of authority and infallibility of anyone until he presents his credentials. Jesus Christ presents His credentials.

First of all, Jesus presents the credential of the divine life that He lived. What do they have in comparison with that? We hear much about the beauty of the life of some who belong to this school of critics. We have no desire to deny the claim, but we gladly put the life of Jesus against the beauty of their lives. Which suffers by the comparison? If there is any force in the argument, "If a man's life is in the right, his doctrine cannot be in the wrong" (and there is force in that argument), it bears immeasurably more for the authority of Jesus Christ than it does for the authority of any critic or school of critics.

> We do not yield to the claim of authority and infallibility of anyone until he presents his credentials. Jesus Christ presents His credentials.

Second, Jesus presents the credential of the divine words that He spoke. What do they have to put up against that? The words of Jesus Christ have stood the test of twenty centuries, and they shine with greater brilliance and glory today than ever. What school of criticism has ever stood the test of even twenty years? If one has to choose between the teaching of Christ and that of any school of criticism, it will not take any thoroughly sane person long to choose.

Third, Jesus Christ presents His credential of the divine works that He did, the unmistakable seal of God upon His claims. What does this school of criticism have to put up against that? Absolutely nothing. It has no miracles except miracles of literary ingenuity in the attempt to make the preposterous appear historical.

Fourth, Jesus Christ presents the credential of His influence upon human history. We all know what the influence of Jesus Christ has been, how beneficial and how divine. Everything that is best in modern civilization, everything that is best in national, domestic, and individual life, is due to the influence of Jesus Christ.

We also know the influence of this school of criticism. We know that it is weakening the power of ministers and Christian workers everywhere. We know that it is emptying churches. We know that it is depleting missionary funds. We know that it is paralyzing missionary effort on every field where it has gone. I know this by personal observation, and not by mere hearsay. This may not be their intention, and with some of them it is not their intention, but nonetheless, it is a fact. The influence of Jesus has been thoroughly beneficial, while the influence of this school of criticism is completely unhelpful.

Fifth, Jesus presents the credential of His resurrection from the dead. What does this school of criticism have to set up against that? Nothing whatsoever! Jesus

Christ establishes His claim. The opposing school of criticism stands silent.

Therefore, we refuse to bow to the assumed and unsubstantiated authority and infallibility of any school of criticism, of any priest, pope, or theological professor, but most gladly do we bow to the authority and infallibility of Jesus Christ, so completely proven. Upon His authority we accept the entire Old Testament and the entire New Testament as the Word of God.

Chapter 2

Two More Reasons Why I Believe That the Bible Is the Word of God

In the first chapter, we saw that if we accepted the authority of Jesus Christ, we must accept the entire Old Testament and the entire New Testament because He set the stamp of His authority on both. It is either Christ and the whole Bible, or no Bible and no Christ.

My second reason for believing that the Bible is the Word of God is because of its fulfilled prophecies. The average unbeliever knows absolutely nothing about fulfilled prophecy, and this is not to be wondered at, for the average Christian knows nothing about fulfilled prophecy. Even the average preacher knows practically nothing about fulfilled prophecy. The subject of prophecy is a large one, and to go into it thoroughly would take many chapters, but it can be presented in an outline in a few moments with sufficient fullness to show the overwhelming weight of the argument.

There are two kinds of prophecy in the Bible: there are the explicit, verbal prophecies, and there are prophecies of types and symbols.

We will first discuss the explicit, verbal prophecies. These are of three kinds:

1. Prophecies regarding the coming Messiah

2. Prophecies regarding the Jewish people

3. Prophecies regarding the gentile nations

We will limit ourselves now to prophecies regarding the coming Messiah. We will only look at five of them by way of illustration: Isaiah 53 (the entire chapter), Micah 5:2, Daniel 9:25-27, Jeremiah 23:5-6, and Psalm 16:8-11.

In the passages listed, we have predictions of a coming king of Israel. We are told the exact time of His manifestation to His people, the exact place of His birth, the family from whom He would be born, and the condition of the family at the time of His birth (a condition entirely different from that existing at the time the prophecy was written, and contrary to all the probabilities in the case). We are told the manner of His reception by His people (a reception entirely different from that which would naturally be expected), the fact, method, and details regarding His death (with the specific circumstances regarding His burial), His resurrection subsequent to His burial, and His victory subsequent to His resurrection. Jesus of Nazareth fulfilled these predictions with the most exact precision.

An attempt has been made by the rationalists to show

that Isaiah 53 does not refer to the coming Messiah. It is natural that they would attempt this, for if it does refer to the coming Messiah, the case of the rationalists is hopeless.

It is clear, though, that it does refer to the coming Messiah from the fact that this chapter was taken to be messianic by the Jews themselves until its fulfillment in Jesus of Nazareth. Their unwillingness to accept Him as the Messiah drove them into the attempt to show that it was not messianic. Furthermore, the desperate straits to which those who deny its messianic application are driven shows the hopelessness of their case. When asked who the suffering One of Isaiah 53 is if He is not the Messiah, the best answer they can give is that it refers to suffering Israel. However, anyone who carefully reads the passage will see that this interpretation is impossible.

> The desperate straits to which those who deny its messianic application are driven shows the hopelessness of their case.

The sufferer of Isaiah 53 is represented as suffering for the sins of others rather than for His own sins, and those for whom He is suffering are represented as "My people," Israel (verse 8). If the sufferer is suffering for the sins of others rather than for His own, and the others for whom He is suffering are Israel, then surely the sufferer Himself cannot be Israel.

You can bring the prophecies cited down to the very latest date to which the most daring destructive critic ever thought of assigning them, and they are still hundreds of years before the birth of Jesus of Nazareth. How are we going to account for the fact that this Book has the power of looking hundreds of years into the future and predicting with most precise details things to come to pass, then, and that these predictions are fulfilled to the very letter? These are facts that demand to be accounted for.

Some of you are businesspeople. Theologians might weave their theories out of their own inner consciousness without regard to facts, but businesspeople must face facts, and here are facts. There is only one rational explanation of this. Any book that has the power of looking hundreds of years into the future and predicting with exact precision as to person, place, time, and circumstances, detailed things to occur at that remote period, must have for its author the only person in the universe who knows the end from the beginning – God.

Of course, it is quite possible for a farseeing man to look a few years into the future, and by studying causes now observable, predict in a general way some things that will occur. This is not at all how it is with the Bible, though. It is not just a few years into the future, but hundreds of years into the future. The prophecies are not general, but contain precise and specific details. It is not about things that had observable and discernible causes at the time of the prophecy, but the causes were not discernible at the time, yet these predictions were fulfilled to the letter. To a mind willing to bow to facts and their necessary meaning, it is conclusive evidence of the divine origin of the Book.

A noteworthy fact regarding the prophecies of the

Bible is that there are often two seemingly contradictory lines of prophecy, and it seems that if the one line of prophecy were fulfilled, the other could not be, yet these two seemingly contradictory lines of prophecy converge and are fulfilled in one Person. For example, in the Old Testament we have two lines of prophecy concerning the Messiah. One line predicts a suffering Messiah, *despised and rejected of men, a man of sorrows and acquainted with grief*, whose earthly mission will end in death and shame. The other line of prophecy predicts with equal clearness and definiteness an all-conquering Messiah who will rule the nations with a rod of iron.

How can both lines of prophecy be true? Before the fulfillment of both lines in Jesus Christ, the best answer the ancient Jew had was that there were to be two Messiahs: one a suffering Messiah of the tribe of Joseph, and one a conquering Messiah of the tribe of Judah. However, in the actual fulfillment, both lines of prophecy meet in the one Person, Jesus of Nazareth. At His first coming He was the suffering Messiah, making atonement for sin by His death upon the cross, as was so often predicted in the Old Testament. At His second coming He will come as a conquering king to rule the nations.

The prophecies of the types and symbols are even more conclusive than the specific verbal prophecies. If you ask the ordinary, superficial student of the Bible how much of the Old Testament is prophetic, he will reply something like this: "Isaiah, Jeremiah, Ezekiel, Daniel, and the Minor Prophets are prophetic." He might add that there are also prophetic passages here and there in the Psalms and Pentateuch.

However, if you asked a serious student of the Bible how much of the Old Testament is prophetic, he will tell you that the entire book is prophetic, that its history is prophetic, that its people are prophetic, and that its institutions, ceremonies, offerings, and feasts are prophetic. If you are skeptical (as you have a right to be until you have investigated, but you have no right to remain doubtful unless you do investigate), but will take time, he will sit down and take you through the whole Book from the first chapter of Genesis to the last chapter of Malachi, and will show you unmistakable foreshadowings of things to come everywhere.

He will show you unquestionable foreshadowings of the truth regarding Christ in the lives of Abraham, Isaac, Joseph, David, and Solomon. He will show you the same thing in every sacrifice and offering, in every feast, in every institution, in the tabernacle and in every part of the tabernacle, in its outer court, in the Holy Place and Most Holy Place, in the brazen altar, in the golden candlestick, in the table of showbread, in the golden altar of incense, in the veil that hung between the Holy Place and Most Holy Place, in the ark of the covenant, in its boards, bars, sockets, and tenons, and in the very coverings of the tabernacle. In all these he will show you that every truth about Christ is clearly set forth – His Person, His nature, His character, His atoning death, His resurrection, His ascension, and His coming again. He will show that Jesus Christ is set forth in all the facts of Jewish and Christian history.

He will show you that every profound truth that was to be fully revealed in the New Testament was prefigured in the types and symbols of the Old Testament. At first, this might seem to you to be just a fortunate coincidence, but as you go on verse after verse, chapter after chapter, and book after book, if you are a fair-minded person, you will be overwhelmingly convinced that this was the thought and intention of the real Author.

As you see all the profoundest truths of Christian doctrine set forth in this ancient history and in this legislation that was established to meet the immediate needs of the people, and as you see the perfect foreshadowing of all the facts of the history of Christ, the Jewish people, and the church, you will be driven to recognize in it the mind and wisdom of God. The modern critical theories regarding the construction of Exodus, Leviticus, Numbers, and Deuteronomy go all to pieces when considered in the light of the meaning of the types of the Old Testament. I have never known a destructive critic who knew anything to speak of regarding the types. One cannot study them thoroughly without being profoundly convinced that the real Author of the Old Testament, the one behind the human authors, is God.

> One cannot study them thoroughly without being profoundly convinced that the real Author of the Old Testament, the one behind the human authors, is God.

My third reason for believing that the Bible is the Word of God is because of the unity of the Book. This is an old argument, but a good one. The Bible is composed, as I suppose you know, of sixty-six parts or books. It is often said that the Bible is not a book, but a library. This is partly true and partly false. It is true that the Bible is a library, but at the same time it is the most profoundly unified single book of any book in existence.

The sixty-six books that compose the Bible were written by at least forty different authors. They were written in three different languages – Hebrew, Aramaic, and Greek. The books were composed over a period of at least fifteen hundred years. They were written in countries hundreds of miles apart. They were written by men upon every plane of political and social life, from the king upon the throne down to the herdsman, shepherd, fisherman, and the petty politician.

The books of the Bible display every form of literary structure. In the Bible we find all kinds of poetry – epic poetry, lyric poetry, didactic poetry, romantic poetry, elegy, and rhapsody. We find all kinds of prose as well – historic prose, didactic prose, theological treatise, epistle, proverb, parable, allegory, and oration.

In a book so composite, made up of such divergent parts, composed at such remote periods of time, and under such diverse circumstances, we would naturally expect variance, discord, and utter lack of unity. In point of fact, though, what do we find? We find the most marvelous unity. Every part of the Bible fits every other part of the Bible. One ever-increasing, ever-growing thought pervades the whole. The character of this unity is most significant. It is not a superficial unity, but it is a profound and thorough unity.

On the surface, we often find apparent discrepancy and disagreement, but as we study, the apparent discrepancy and disagreement disappear, and the deep underlying unity appears. The more deeply we study, the more complete we find the unity to be.

The unity is also an organic one; that is, it is not the unity of a lifeless thing, like a stone, but of a living thing, like a plant. In the early books of the Bible, we have the developing thought. As we continue, we have the plant. Further on, we have the bud, and then the blossom, and then the ripened fruit. In Revelation, we find the ripened fruit of Genesis.

How are we to account for it? This is another fact that demands accounting for, and as businesspeople, you have to deal with facts, not theories. You must deal with realities, and not finespun speculations of cloistered theologians who spend their time dreaming apart from the substantial realities of life. There is one easy and simple way to account for it, and only one rational way to account for it at all, and that is that behind the forty or more human authors was the one all-governing, all-controlling, all-superintending, all-shaping mind of God.

Suppose it were proposed to build in Washington, D.C. a temple that would represent the stone products from every State in the Union. Some stones would come from the marble quarries of Marlboro, New Hampshire, others from the granite quarries of Quincy,

Massachusetts, some from the brownstone quarries of Middletown, Connecticut, some from the white marble quarries at Rutland, Vermont, some from the grey sandstone quarries at Berea, Ohio, some from the porphyry quarries below Knoxville, Tennessee, some from the red-stone quarries near Hancock, Michigan, some from the brown-stone quarries at Kasota, Minnesota, some from the gypsum quarries of the far west – some stones from every state in the Union.

The stones were to be of all conceivable sizes and shapes. Some would be large, some small, and some medium. Some were to be cubical, some spherical, some cylindrical, some conical, some trapezoidal, and some rectangular parallelograms. Each stone was to be hewn into its final shape at the quarry from which it was taken. Not a stone was to be touched by mallet or chisel after it reached its destination.

Finally, the stones are at Washington, and the builders go to work. As they build, they find that every stone fits into every other stone, each into its place. It is found that there is not one stone too many, or one stone too few, until at last the builders' work is done and there rises before you a temple with its side walls, its buttresses, its naves, its arches, its hallways, its roof, its pinnacles, and its dome perfect in every outline and in every detail. There is not one stone too many and not one stone too few. There is not one stone left over, and there is no niche or corner where one stone is lacking, yet every stone had been hewn into its final shape in the quarry from which it was taken. How would you account for it?

There is one very simple way to account for it, and only one way to account for it at all, and that is that behind the individual quarry workers was a master architect who planned the whole building from the beginning and gave to each individual quarryman his specifications for the work.

This is precisely what we find in that temple of eternal truth that we call the Bible. The stones for this Book were quarried in places remote from one another by hundreds of miles, and at periods of time fifteen hundred years apart. There were stones of all conceivable sizes and shapes, and yet every stone fits into its place and fits with every other stone, until when the Book is finished there rises before you this matchless temple of God's truth, perfect in every outline and every detail. There is not one stone too many or one stone too few, and yet every stone was cut into its final shape in the quarry from which it was taken.

How are you to account for it? There is only one rational way to account for it, and that is that behind the human hands that worked was the mastermind of God who thought and gave to each individual workman his specifications for the work. You cannot get around that and be honest and fair.

Chapter 3

Four More Reasons Why
I Believe That the Bible
Is the Word of God

I have given you three reasons so far why I believe that the Bible is the Word of God. First, because of the testimony of Jesus Christ to that effect. The second reason was because of its fulfilled prophecies. The third reason for believing that the Bible is the Word of God was because of the unity of the Book.

My fourth reason for believing the Bible to be the Word of God is because of the immeasurable superiority of its teachings to those of any other or all other books. It was quite popular when I was studying in theological halls to compare the teachings of the Bible with those of cultural seers and philosophers, such as the teachings of Socrates, Plato, Marcus Aurelius Antonius, Epictetus, Isocrates, Seneca, Buddha,

Zoroaster, Confucius, Mencius, and Mohammed. This is getting to be popular again. Anyone who institutes such a comparison and puts the Bible in the same class with these other teachers must be either ignorant of the teachings of the Bible, ignorant of the teachings of these ethnic seers and philosophers, or what is more frequently the case, ignorant of both. There are three points of radical difference between the teachings of the Bible and those of any other book.

First, these other teachers contain truth, but it is truth mixed with error. The Bible contains nothing but truth. There are gems of thought in these other writers, but as Joseph Cook said years ago, they are "jewels picked out of the mud." For example, we are often asked: "Did not Socrates teach most beautifully how a philosopher ought to die?" He did, but they forget to tell us that he also taught a woman of the town how to conduct her business that was not quite so nice.

We are also asked, "Did not Marcus Aurelius Antonius teach most excellently about clemency?" He did. It is well worth reading, but they forget to tell us that he also taught that it was right to put people to death for no other crime than that of being Christians, and being himself emperor of Rome, and having power to do it, he practiced what he preached. "Did not Seneca," they ask, "speak wonderfully about the advantages of poverty?" He did, but they forget to tell us that Seneca himself was at the time one of the worst spendthrifts in Rome, the onyx tables alone in his mansion costing a fabulous fortune. Moreover, he was the tutor under whose influence the most infamous emperor that Rome ever had, Nero, was brought up.

"Did not Confucius," they ask, "admirably explain the duty of children to parents?" He did, but they forget to tell us that Confucius also taught that it was right to tell lies on occasion, and he unblushingly tells us that he himself lied at times. There is perhaps nothing in which his most devoted followers have followed so closely in the footsteps of their great master as in this matter of lying. They have reduced lying to a fine art, and they will say anything "to save face."

The second point of difference is that these other writings contain part of the truth, while the Bible contains all the truth. There is not a single known truth on moral or spiritual subjects that cannot be found within the covers of the Bible. This is a most remarkable fact. The Bible is an old Book, and yet man in all his thinking before and since the Bible was written has not discovered one single truth on moral or spiritual subjects that cannot be found for substance within the covers of the Bible.

> If all other books were destroyed and the Bible alone remained, we would suffer no essential loss on moral and spiritual subjects.

In other words, if all other books were destroyed and the Bible alone remained, we would suffer no essential loss on moral and spiritual subjects. However, if the Bible were destroyed and all other books remained, the loss would be irreparable. If the Bible were just another book written by men, why would this be? I have often challenged anyone in my audiences to bring forward one single truth on moral or spiritual subjects that I could not find within the Bible. It is quite conceivable that someone might succeed in doing this, for I do not pretend to know everything that is in the Bible. I have only been studying it a little over a quarter of a century. However, no one has been able to meet the challenge yet.

The third point of radical difference is that the Bible contains more truth than all other books put together. You can go to all literature, ancient and modern, including the literature of ancient Greece, ancient Rome, ancient India, ancient Persia, ancient China, and all modern literature, pull out of it all that is good, throw away all that is bad or worthless, bring together the result of your labor into one book, and even then you will not have a book that will take the place of this one Book. If the Bible is just another book written by men, why is it that in all the thousands of years of men's thinking, and in all the millions of books they have produced, that they have not been able, in all of those books put together, to produce as much real and priceless wisdom as is contained in this one Book? The answer is plain: other books are men's books, while the Bible stands alone as God's Book.

My fifth reason for believing the Bible to be the Word of God is because of the history of the Book and its omnipotence against all men's attacks. What man has made, man can destroy. However, twenty centuries of the most strenuous and determined assault have been unable to destroy or undermine intelligent faith in the Bible.

The Bible had only just been given to the world before people discovered three things about it. First, they learned that it condemned sin. Second, they saw that it demanded renunciation of self. Third, they observed that it laid human pride in the dust. People were not willing to give up sin, they were not willing to renounce self, and they were not willing to have their pride laid in the dust. Therefore, they hated the Book that made these demands.

People's hatred of the Bible has been most intense and most active. They determined to destroy the Book that they hated. Man after man has arisen with the determination to destroy this Book. Celsus tried it with the brilliancy of his genius, and he failed. Then Porphyry tried it with the depth of his philosophy, and he failed. Lucien tried it with the keenness of his satire, and he failed.

Then Diocletian came on the scene and tried other weapons. He brought to bear against the Bible all the military and political power of the strongest empire the world had ever known at the height of its glory. He issued edicts that every Bible should be burned, but that failed. Stronger edicts were issued, that those who owned Bibles should be put to death, and that failed.

For twenty centuries, the attack upon the Bible has continued. Every method of destruction that human wisdom, human science, human philosophy, human intelligence, human satire, human force, and human brutality could bring to bear against a book have been brought to bear against this Book, and the Bible still stands. At times, nearly all the great rulers of earth have been against it with only an obscure remnant for it, but still the Bible has more than held its own.

Today it has a firmer hold upon the confidence and affections of the best and wisest men and women than it ever had before in the world's history. If the Bible had been a mere human book, it would have gone down and would have been forgotten centuries ago, but because there is in this Book not only the hiding of God's wisdom, but the hiding of His power, it has wonderfully fulfilled the words of Jesus: *Heaven and earth shall pass away, but My words shall not pass away* (Matthew 24:35).

> **If the Bible had been a mere human book, it would have gone down and would have been forgotten centuries ago.**

Amid the deafening roar of the enemies' artillery and the dense smoke of battle, it has seemed to some people at times as if the Bible was going to fall, but when the smoke has rolled away from the field of conflict, this invincible citadel of God's eternal truth has reared its lofty head heavenward, unscathed, without one stone dislodged from foundation to highest tower. Each new assault upon the Bible has simply served to illustrate anew the absolute omnipotence of this God-given Book.

In a way, I rejoice in every new attack that is made upon the Bible. I tremble for certain weak-minded men and women who are willing to believe anything that they are assured is the consensus of the latest scholarship, but for the Bible itself I have no fears. A Book that has successfully withstood twenty centuries of assault of the devil's heaviest artillery is not going down before the air guns of modern criticism.

My sixth reason for believing that the Bible is the Word of God is because of the influence of the Book and its power to lift people up to God. Every honest person must see and admit that there is a power in this Book to brighten and gladden and beautify and dignify human lives, to lift people up to God, that no other book possesses. A stream can rise no higher than its source, and a Book that has power to lift people up to God that no other book possesses must have come down from God in a way that no other book has.

In literally millions of cases, this Book has demonstrated its power to reach down to men and women in the deepest depths of iniquity and degradation and lift them up, up, up, until they were fit for a place beside Christ upon the throne. I remember a man who had a brilliant mind, but was dismayed and corrupted and demonized by alcohol, and this man was an agnostic. I urged him to accept the Bible and the Christ of the Bible, but with a hollow laugh he said, "I don't believe in your Bible or your Christ. I am an agnostic." In the end, though, sunken to the lowest depths of ruin, he threw his agnosticism to the winds and accepted this Book and the Christ of this Book, and by the power of this Book was transformed into one of the truest, noblest, humblest men I know. What other book could do this?

This Book has power, not only to lift individuals,

but nations, toward God. We owe all that is best in our modern civilization, in our political, commercial, and domestic life, to the influence of this Book. The person who attacks the Book is attacking the very foundation of all that is best in modern civilization. The person who attacks the Bible is the worst enemy that an individual or society has.

The seventh reason as to why I believe that the Bible is the Word of God is because of the character of those who accept it as such, and because of the character of those who reject it. Two things speak for the divine origin of this Book: the character of those who are sure that it is the Word of God, and the character of those who deny it.

Often when some man or woman says to me, "I firmly believe that the Bible is the Word of God," and when I look at the purity, the beauty, the humility, and the devotion to God and man that there is in their character, and how near they live to God, I feel like saying, "I am glad that you believe that the Bible is the Word of God. The fact that someone who lives so near God and knows God as well as you do believes the Bible to be His Book is a confirmation of my own faith that it is."

On the other hand, often when a man or woman with a self-confident toss of the head says, "I do not believe that the Bible is the Word of God," and when I look at the sinfulness or selfishness or pettiness or lowness of their lives and how far they live from God, I feel like saying, "I am glad that you do not. The fact that a person who is living upon the plane that you are living, living so far from God and knowing God so little, doubts that the Bible is the Word of God, is a confirmation of my own faith that it is."

Do not misunderstand me. I do not mean by this that everyone who professes to believe in the Bible is better than everyone who rejects the Bible, but what I do mean is this: show me a person who is living a life of absolute surrender to God, living under the control of the Spirit of God, living a life of devotion to the highest welfare of his fellow men, a life of humility and of prayer, and I will show you every time a person who believes the Bible to be God's Word.

On the other hand, show me someone who denies or persistently questions that the Bible is the Word of God, and I will show you someone who is leading either (mind you, I say "either," not "all") a life of greed for gold, or of lust, or of self-will, or of spiritual pride. I challenge anyone to provide me an exception. I have been looking for one literally around the world, and I have never found one. An attempt to furnish an exception has been made a number of times, but it is simply laughable to think of the people suggested to me as leading lives of humility and prayer, or to think of them as not leading lives of "self-will." Anyone who has not absolutely surrendered to God is leading a life of self-will.

In other words, all who live nearest God and know God best are sure that the Bible is God's Word. Those who have the most doubts about it are those who are living farthest from God and know God least. Which people will you believe?

Suppose that a manuscript was discovered in the city of Boston that was professed to be by Oliver Wendell Holmes, but that there was great discussion among the critics as to whether or not Oliver Wendell Holmes was the real author. Finally it was submitted to a committee of critics for decision, and it was discovered that all those critics who knew Oliver Wendell Holmes best, who lived in most intimate fellowship with him, and who were most in sympathy with his thought were absolutely unanimous in their declaration that the manuscript was by him. However, those who questioned it were those who knew Oliver Wendell Holmes the least, had the least fellowship with him, and were least in sympathy with his thought. Which group would you believe?

That is a very simple question in literary criticism, much simpler than that which our modern critics so confidently undertake to solve, such as who may be the seven different authors of a single verse in a book written thousands of years ago, as is attempted in that monumental jokebook of the nineteenth century, the Polychrome Bible. This is the precise case with the Bible. All who live nearest God and know God best, all who are in most intimate fellowship with Him, are of absolutely one accord in saying that the Bible is His work. Those who have the most doubts about it are those who live farthest from Him and know God least.

There is another significant fact, and that is that the nearer people get to God, the more confident they become that the Bible is His Word. The farther they drift from God, the more doubts enter their hearts. It constantly happens that someone who is a sinner and an unbeliever gives up his sin without further argument and is also delivered from his unbelief. Can anyone provide one single instance of the opposite kind, where someone was a sinner and a believer, and by giving up his sin lost his faith?

Furthermore, it often occurs that someone who was living a life of consecration and of nearness to God, and who enjoyed a serene and undisturbed faith that the Bible was God's Word, begins to prosper in the things of this world, and the love of money enters his heart. He then drifts away from outright separation of his life to God, and as he drifts from God, he drifts into doubt and into careless views about the Bible. We see this today all around us. People who become careless in their morals also become careless in their doctrine. Broad morals and broad theology go hand in hand. They are twin brothers.

> People who become careless in their morals also become careless in their doctrine.

This is so true that often when people tell me that they are starting to doubt, I ask them the question, "What have you been doing?" Once while walking in a university town, I saw a little way ahead of me on the street a young fellow whom I knew. I caught up with him and said to him, "Charlie, how are you getting on?" With a self-satisfied look, he said, "Well, to tell you the truth, Mr. Torrey, I am becoming somewhat skeptical."

I said, "Charlie, what have you been doing?" The poor fellow blushed and dropped his head. Charlie had been sinning, and sin had brought doubt. This is the history of the beginning of doubt in the hearts of thousands of people today.

Where is the stronghold of the Bible? The stronghold of the Bible is the pure, happy, unselfish home. Where is the stronghold of unbelief? The stronghold of unbelief is the tavern, the racetrack, the gambling hell, and the brothel. Suppose that I would come as a stranger to your city. Suppose I would enter one of your taverns with a Bible under my arm, lay my Bible down upon the bar, and order a glass of whiskey, adding, "Make it big." What would happen? There would be much surprise.

The bartender would quite likely say, "Excuse me, but what is that book? Isn't that the Bible?"

"Yes."

"And what did you ask for – whiskey?"

"Yes, and make it large."

He would not know what to make of it. However, suppose I would enter the tavern and lay upon the bar a copy of any work of an atheist like Ingersoll or of Bradlaugh, or a copy of the *Clarion*, or the *Agnostic Journal*, or the *Freethinker*, or the most respectable atheist book or paper that there is, and order a glass of whiskey. I would get it without a question or a look of surprise. It would be just what they would expect. The Bible and whiskey don't go together. Unbelief and whiskey do go together.

I told this story when I was in Belfast, and at the close of the address a physician came to me laughing. He said, "Just yesterday we had an illustration of just what you said. After your afternoon Bible reading, my mother went into a store to get some brandy for a friend who was ill. She had her Bible in her hand, and without thinking of how it looked, was trying to put it into the bag that she carried. The clerk who was waiting upon her said, 'That is right, madam; hide it. The two don't go well together.'"

Chapter 4

Three More Reasons Why
I Believe That the Bible
Is the Word of God

In the three previous chapters, I have given you seven reasons why I believe the Bible is the Word of God. In this chapter, I will give you three more reasons.

My eighth reason for believing that the Bible is the Word of God is because of the inexhaustible depth of the Book. What man has produced, man can exhaust. However, twenty centuries of study on the part of tens of thousands of the ablest minds have been unable to exhaust the Bible. Many men of strongest intellect, of marvelous powers of penetration, and of broadest culture have given a lifetime to the study of the Bible, and no one who has really studied it has ever dreamed of saying that he has gotten to the bottom of the Book. Indeed, the more profoundly one digs into the Book, the more clearly he sees that there are still unfathomable depths of wisdom beneath him in this inexhaustible mine of truth.

Not only is this true of individuals, but it is also true of generations of men. Thousands of men in cooperation with one another have delved into this mine, but so far from exhausting it, there are still new treasures of truth awaiting each new student of the Word. New light is constantly breaking forth from the Word of God. How are we to account for this unquestionable fact?

The human mind has been progressing during these twenty centuries. We have outgrown every other book that belongs to the past, but so far from outgrowing the Bible, we have not grown up to it. The Bible is not only up-to-date, but it is always ahead of date. The best interpretation of the most recent events of our own day is found in this old Book. If this Book were man's book, we would have gotten to the bottom of it centuries ago, but the fact that it has proved itself unfathomable for twenty centuries is positive proof that the infinite treasures of the wisdom and knowledge of God are hidden in it.

A brilliant Unitarian writer in America has given utterance to one of the keenest sentences that was ever spoken or written from the standpoint of the denial of the inspiration of the Bible. He said, "How irreligious to accuse an infinite God of having put His whole wisdom in one Book that is so small!" I submit that that is cutting, but this writer did not see how the sharp edge of his Damascus blade could be turned against himself. What a testimony to the divine origin of this

Book that such infinite wisdom can be packed in such a small area!

The Bible is not really a very large book (I have a copy that I carry in my vest pocket), yet that small Book contains such treasures of wisdom that twenty centuries of study by the world's best minds have been unable to exhaust it. How are we to explain this? There is no one except God who could pack such infinite treasures of truth in such a small area.

My ninth reason for believing that the Bible is the Word of God is the fact that as I grow in knowledge and in character, in wisdom and in holiness, I grow toward the Bible. The nearer I get to God, the nearer I get to the Bible. When I began to really study the Bible, I had the same experience with it that every careful student has had in the beginning of his studies. I found things in the Bible that were difficult to understand, and other things that seemed difficult to believe. I found that the teachings of one part of the Book

> There is no one except God who could pack such infinite treasures of truth in such a small area.

seemed to flatly contradict the teachings of other parts of the Book. It seemed clear to me that if one teaching of the Bible were true, some other teaching of the Bible could not be. Like so many others, I accepted as much of the Bible as was wise enough to agree with me.

As I continued to study the Bible, and as I continued growing in likeness to God, I found that my difficulties were disappearing. At first, they went away one by one, then by twos, and then by dozens, ever disappearing more and more. I constantly found that the nearer I got to God, the nearer I got to the Bible. What is the inevitable mathematical conclusion? Two lines always converging as they draw near to a given point must meet when they reach that point. The nearer I got to God, the nearer I got to the Bible. When God and I meet, the Bible and I will meet. That is, the Bible was written from God's standpoint. There is no honest escaping of this conclusion.

Suppose I were to pass through a vast, dark, and dangerous forest for the first time. Before starting upon this perilous tour, a guide was brought to me who had often been through the forest and had conducted many people through in safety, and he had never led a single person astray. Under his guidance, I began my journey through the forest. We got on very nicely together for a while, but after a time we came to a place where two roads diverged. The guide said to me, "The path to the right is the right path to take."

However, my judgment and reason, according to what I could observe, indicated to me that the road to the left was the road to take. I said to the guide, "I know that you have been through this forest many times and that you have safely led many people through. Because of this, I have great confidence in your judgment, but in the present instance I believe you are wrong. My reason and judgment, according to what I observe, clearly indicates to me that the road to the left is the road to take. I have never been through this forest before, and you have, and I know that my reason and judgment are not infallible, but they are the best guide that I have, and I cannot disregard them. I must follow them."

So I take the road to the left. I go about a mile and then come to an impassable bog, and I have to go back and take the way the guide said. We get on well together again for a ways, but again we come to a place where two paths diverge. This time the guide says, "The road to the left is the road to take." But my reason and judgment based upon my observation clearly indicates that the road to the right is the road to take, and again we have our little discussion.

I say to the guide, "I know that you have often passed through this forest and have never led anyone astray. I have great confidence in your judgment, but my reason and common sense based upon my observation tell me that the road to the right is the road to take. Now I know that my reason and common sense are not infallible, but they are the best guide that I have, and I cannot disregard them."

So again I take the other path. I go about half a mile, and then run up against an impassable barrier of rock. I have to go back and go the way the guide said. Suppose that this would happen fifty times, and every time the guide was right, and my reason and common sense based upon what I observed through my senses proved wrong. Do you not think that about the fifty-first time I would have reason and common sense enough to throw my ever-erring judgment to the winds and go the way the guide said?

This has been my exact experience with the Bible. Time and time again I have come to the parting of the ways, where the Bible said one thing and my reason and common sense seemed to say another. The fool that I was, I disregarded the Bible and went the way that my reason and common sense said, and every time I have had to come back and go the way the Bible said. I hope that the next time I and the Bible differ, I will have common sense enough to disregard my ever-erring reason and judgment and go the way the Bible says.

The most irrational thing in the world is what we call rationalism. Rationalism is an attempt to subject the teachings of infinite wisdom to the criticism of our finite judgment. Could anything possibly be more irrational than that? It never seems to occur to the rationalist that God can have a good reason for saying or doing a thing if he, the rationalist, cannot see the reason. One of the greatest discoveries that I ever made was one day when it dawned upon me that God might possibly know more than I did, and that God might possibly be right, when to me He appeared to be wrong.

My tenth reason for believing the Bible to be the Word of God is because of the testimony of the Holy Spirit to that fact. To the one who puts himself in the right attitude toward God and truth, the Holy Spirit bears direct testimony that the voice that speaks to him from the Bible is the voice of God.

One will often meet a godly old woman who is not very widely read or cultured, who still has a firm faith that the Bible is the Word of God. If you ask her why she believes that the Bible is the Word of God, she will reply, "I know that the Bible is the Word of God." If you ask her again, "Why do you believe it is the Word of God?" she will reply, "I know it is the Word of God." If you ask yet again, "Why do you believe it is the Word of God?" again she will reply, "I know it is the Word of God." Very likely you will say, "Well, I will not disturb the old lady's faith (have no fear, for you couldn't even if you wanted to), but she is beyond argument." You are mistaken, for she is above argument.

Jesus Christ said, *He that is of God heareth God's words* (John 8:47). Jesus Christ also said, *My sheep hear My voice* (John 10:27). That woman is one of God's children and knows her Father's voice, and she knows that the voice that speaks to her from the Bible is the voice of God. She is one of Christ's sheep, and she knows that the voice that speaks to her from the Bible is the voice of the true Shepherd.

> There is nothing that so clarifies the human mind as the surrender of the will to God.

I can tell any of you how you can come to that same place where you will be able to distinguish God's voice and to know that the voice that speaks to you from the Bible is the voice of God. Jesus Christ Himself tells us this in John 7:17: *If any man willeth to do His will, he shall know of the teaching whether it be of God, or whether I speak from Myself.* The surrender of the will to God opens the eyes of the soul to see the truth of God. Jesus Christ does not demand that we believe without evidence, but He does demand that we put ourselves in that moral attitude toward God and the truth that makes us competent to appreciate evidence.

There is nothing that so clarifies the human mind as the surrender of the will to God.

Some years ago I was lecturing to our students in Chicago on how to deal with skeptics and unbelievers. Our lecture room in Chicago is open to people of all kinds and conditions, and it is often a varied crowd that gathers together: Christian and Jew, Roman Catholic and Protestant, believers, skeptics, unbelievers, agnostics, and atheists. At the close of this lecture, the wife of the late Dr. A. J. Gordon of Boston came to me and said, "Did you see the man sitting near me as you spoke?" I had noticed the man because I had had a little conversation with him before. "Well," she added, "while you were speaking, I heard him say, 'I wish he would try it upon me.'"

"I would be glad to," I said.

"Well, there he is over in the corner." I did not need to go to him, for when the other people had left, he came to me and said, "Mr. Torrey, I do not want to say anything discourteous, but my experience contradicts everything that you have said to these students this morning."

I replied, "Have you done what I told these students to get the infidel or skeptic to do, and guaranteed that if they would do it they would come out of their doubt and unbelief and into a clear faith in the Bible as the Word of God and Jesus as the Son of God?"

"Yes, I have done it all."

"Now," I said, "let's be certain about this."

I called my secretary over and dictated something like this: "I believe that there is an absolute difference between right and wrong" (I did not say, "I believe that there is a God," for this man was an agnostic and neither affirmed nor denied the existence of God, and you have to begin where someone is), "and I hereby take my stand upon the right to follow it wherever it carries me. I promise to make an honest search to find if Jesus Christ is the Son of God, and if I find that He is, I promise to accept Him as my Savior and confess Him publicly before the world."

My secretary brought two copies of this, and I handed them to him and said, "Are you willing to sign this?"

He replied, "Certainly," and he signed them both. He folded one and put it in his pocket. I folded the other and put it in my pocket. Then he added, "There is nothing in it. My case is very unusual." (His case was indeed unusual. He had been through Unitarianism, spiritualism, theosophy, and pretty much all other "isms," and was now an open agnostic.)

"Another thing," I added. "Do you know for sure that there is not a God?"

"No," he said. "I don't know that there is not a God. Anyone would be a fool to say he knows that there is not a God. I am an agnostic. I neither affirm nor deny."

I said, "Well, I know that there is a God, but that won't do you any good. Do you know that God does not answer prayer?"

"No. I do not know that God does not answer prayer. I do not believe that He answers prayer, but I do not know that He does not answer prayer."

"Well," I said, "I know that He does answer prayer, but that will not do you any good. However, here is a possible clue to knowledge. You are a graduate of a British university, aren't you?"

"Yes."

"You know the method of modern science, don't you? The method of modern science is that if one finds a possible clue to knowledge, he should follow that possible clue to see what there may be in it. Well, here is a possible clue. Will you adopt the methods of modern science in religious investigation? Will you follow out this possible clue to see what there may be in it? Will you offer the following prayer? 'Oh God, if there is any God, show me if Jesus Christ is Your Son or not, and if You show me that He is Your Son, I promise to accept Him as my Savior and confess Him as such before the world.'"

"Yes," he said. "I will do that, too, but there is nothing in it. My case is very unusual."

"One more thing," I said. "John 20:31 says, *These are written that ye might believe that Jesus is the Christ, the Son of God, and that believing ye might have life through His name.* John tells us here that the Gospel of John was written to show people the proof that Jesus is the Christ, the Son of God. Will you read the proof? Will you read the Gospel of John?"

"I have read it again and again," he replied. "I can quote parts of it to you if you want to hear them."

"No," I said, "but I want you to read it this time in a new way. Each time before you read, offer this prayer: 'Oh God, if there is any God, show me what truth there is in the verses I am about to read, and what You show me to be true, I promise to accept and take my stand upon.' Now, don't read too many verses at a time. Don't try to believe or disbelieve. Simply be open to conviction to the truth. Pay careful attention to what you read, and when you have finished the Gospel, report the result to me."

"Yes," he said. "I will do it all, but there is nothing in it. My case is very unusual."

"Never mind about that," I said. I went over again the three things he had promised to do, and we separated. About two weeks later I was speaking on the south side, and I saw this man in the hall. At the end of the meeting, he came to me and said, "There was something in that."

I replied, "I knew that before."

"Well," he said, "ever since I have done what I promised I would do, it is just as if I had been caught up and was being carried along by the Niagara River, and the first thing I know I will be a shouting Methodist."

I became a Methodist for the occasion and said, "Praise the Lord!" I went east to lecture at some schools in Massachusetts. When I came back, there was a reception, and this man was present at the reception. He came to me and asked, "Are you busy?"

"Not too busy to speak to you," I replied.

We went into another room, and he said, "I cannot understand it. I cannot see how I ever listened to these men" (mentioning a number of infidel and Unitarian writers and speakers). "It is all nonsense to me now."

"Oh," I said, "the Bible explains that in 1 Corinthians 2:14: *The natural man receiveth not the things of the Spirit of God: for they are foolishness unto him: neither can he know them, because they are spiritually discerned.* You have taken the right attitude toward truth, and God has opened your eyes to see the truth."

He came out into a clear faith in Jesus Christ as the Son of God and the Bible as the Word of God. If any of you doubt this story, try it for yourself, and you will have a story of your own to tell.

The Bible is the Word of God. The voice that speaks to us from this Book is the voice of God. Someone will say, "Suppose it is the Word. What of it?" Everything of it! If the Bible is the Word of God, then Jesus Christ is the Son of God, and there is no salvation for any of us outside of a living faith in Him that leads us to put all our trust for pardon in His atoning work on the cross of Calvary and to surrender our wills and our lives absolutely to His control. Have you done this? Will you do it now?

Chapter 5

Did Jesus Christ Really Rise from the Dead?

The resurrection of Jesus Christ is in many respects the most important fact in history. It is the Gibraltar of Christian evidences, the Waterloo of unbelief. If it can be proven to be a historic certainty that Jesus rose from the dead, then Christianity rests upon an invincible foundation. Every essential truth of Christianity is involved in the resurrection. If the resurrection stands, then every essential doctrine of Christianity stands. If the resurrection goes down, then every essential doctrine of Christianity goes down. Intelligent skeptics and atheists realize this.

A leading skeptic has recently said that there is no use wasting time discussing the other miracles. The essential question is, Did Jesus Christ rise from the dead? If He did, it is easy enough to believe the other miracles. If He did not, the other miracles must go. I am confident that this skeptic has correctly stated the case.

There are three separate lines of proof of the truthfulness of the statements contained in the four Gospels regarding the resurrection of Jesus Christ.

First, there is the external evidence for the authenticity and truthfulness of the Gospel narratives. This is a completely satisfactory argument, but we will not enter into it at this time. The argument is long and intricate, and it would take much time to discuss it satisfactorily. The other arguments are so completely sufficient that we can do without this, as good as it is in its place.

The second argument is based upon the internal proofs of the truthfulness of the Gospel records. This argument is absolutely conclusive, and we will proceed to state it briefly. We will not assume anything whatsoever. We will not assume that the four Gospel records are true history. We will not assume that the four Gospels were written by the men whose names they bear. We will not even assume that they were written in the century in which Jesus is alleged to have lived, died, and risen again – nor in the next century, nor in the next. We will assume nothing whatsoever. We will start out with a fact that we all know to be true, and that is that we have the four Gospels today, whoever wrote them. We will place the four Gospels side by side and see if we can recognize in them the marks of truth or of fiction.

The first thing we notice as we compare these Gospels

one with the other is that they are four separate and independent accounts. This appears clearly from the apparent discrepancies in the four different accounts. These apparent discrepancies are obvious and many. It would have been impossible for four accounts to have been made up in collusion with one another and to have so many and so obvious discrepancies in them.

There is a harmony between the four accounts, but the harmony does not lie upon the surface. It only comes out by protracted and thorough study. It is the same kind of harmony that would exist between accounts written by several different people, each looking at the events recorded from his own standpoint. It is just such a harmony that would not exist in four accounts that had been manufactured in collusion. In four accounts manufactured in collusion, whatever harmony there was would have appeared on the surface. Whatever discrepancy there was would only have come out by precise and careful study, but the case is just the opposite. The fact is that the harmony comes out by precise and careful study, while the apparent discrepancy lies upon the surface. Whether true or false, these four accounts are separate and independent from one another. The four accounts supplement one another. A third account sometimes reconciles apparent discrepancies between two others.

It is clear that these accounts must either be a record

> It is clear that these accounts must either be a record of facts that actually occurred, or else they are works of fiction.

of facts that actually occurred, or else they are works of fiction. If fiction, they must have been fabricated in one of two ways: either independently of one another or in collusion with one another. They cannot have been made up independently, for the agreements are too noticeable and too many. They cannot have been made up in collusion, for, as already seen, the apparent discrepancies are too numerous and too noticeable. They were not made up independently and were not made up in collusion. Therefore, it is evident that they were not made up at all. They are a true relation of facts as they actually occurred.

The next thing that we notice is that these accounts bear striking indications of having been derived from eyewitnesses. The account of an eyewitness is easily distinguishable from that of one who is merely retelling what others have told him. Anyone who is accustomed to weigh evidence in court or in historical study soon learns how to distinguish the account of an eyewitness from mere hearsay evidence. Any careful student of the Gospel records of the resurrection will quickly detect many marks of an eyewitness.

Some years ago, when lecturing at an American university, a gentleman was introduced to me as being a skeptic. I asked him what course of study he was pursuing. He replied that he was pursuing a postgraduate course in history with a goal of being a history professor. I said, "Then you know that the account of an eyewitness differs in obvious respects from the account of one who is simply telling what he has heard from others?"

He replied, "Yes."

I then asked, "Have you carefully read the four Gospel accounts of the resurrection of Christ?"

He answered, "I have."

"Tell me, then, have you not noticed clear indications that they were derived from eyewitnesses?"

"Yes," he replied. "I have been greatly struck by this in reading the accounts."

Anyone else who carefully and intelligently reads them will be struck by the same fact.

The third thing that we notice about these Gospel narratives is their naturalness, straightforwardness, genuineness, and simplicity. The accounts indeed have to do with the supernatural, but the accounts themselves are most natural. There is an absolute absence of all attempt at distortion and exaggeration. This is just a simple, straightforward telling of facts as they occurred.

It sometimes happens that a witness on the witness stand tells a story that is so genuine, so straightforward, and so natural, without any attempt at distortion and exaggeration, that his testimony bears weight independently of anything we might know of the character or previous history of the witness. As we listen to his story, we say to ourselves, "This man is telling the truth."

The weight of this kind of evidence is greatly increased and reaches practical certainty when we have several independent witnesses of this sort all bearing testimony to the same essential facts, but with varieties of detail, one omitting what another tells, and the third unconsciously reconciling apparent discrepancies between the two. This is the precise case with the four Gospel narratives of the resurrection of Christ. The Gospel authors do not seem to have reflected at all upon the meaning or manner of many of the facts that they relate. They simply tell outright what they saw, in all simplicity and straightforwardness, leaving the theorizing to others.

Dr. William Furness, the great Unitarian scholar and critic, who certainly was not much disposed in favor of the supernatural, says, "Nothing can exceed in honesty and simplicity the four accounts of the first appearance of Jesus after His crucifixion. If these qualities are not discernible here, we must despair of ever being able to discern them anywhere."

Suppose we would find four accounts of the Battle of Monmouth. Nothing decisive was known as to the authorship of these accounts, but when we laid them side by side, we found that they were clearly independent accounts. We found, furthermore, compelling indications that they were from eyewitnesses. We found them all marked by that honesty, simplicity, and straightforwardness that carry conviction. We found that while they somewhat disagreed in minor details, they agreed substantially in their account of the battle.

Even though we had no knowledge of the authorship or date of these accounts, would we not in the absence of any other account say, "These are true accounts of the Battle of Monmouth"? This is exactly the case with the four Gospel narratives. They are clearly separate and independent from one another, bearing the clear marks of having been derived from eyewitnesses, characterized by an unrivalled genuineness, simplicity, and straightforwardness, seemingly disagreeing in minor details, but in perfect agreement as to the great essential facts related. If we are fair and honest, are we not logically driven to say, "These are true accounts of the resurrection of Jesus"?

The next thing that we notice is the unintentional evidence of words, phrases, and incidental details. It often happens that when a witness is on the stand, the unintentional evidence that he bears by words and phrases that he uses, and by incidental details that he introduces, is more convincing than his direct testimony because it

If the stories were fictitious, they would never have been made up in this way.

is not the testimony of the witness, but the testimony of the truth to itself. The Gospel stories abound in evidence of this sort.

One example is the fact that in all the Gospel records of the resurrection, we are likely to understand that Jesus was not at first recognized by His disciples when He appeared to them after His resurrection (e.g., Luke 24:16; John 21:4). We are not told why this is so, but if we will think about it for a while, we can soon discover why it is so.

However, the Gospel narratives simply record the fact without attempting to explain it. If the stories were fictitious, they would never have been made up in this way, for the writers would have seen at once the objection that would have arisen in the minds of those who did not want to believe in the resurrection – that is, that it was not really Jesus whom the disciples saw.

Why, then, is the story told in this way? It is for the very evident reason that the evangelists were not making the story up for effect, but were recording events precisely as they occurred. This was the way it occurred, and therefore this is the way they told it. It is not a fabrication of imaginary incidents, but an exact record of facts accurately observed and accurately recorded.

Here is a second example. In all the Gospel records of the appearances of Jesus after His resurrection, there is not a single recorded appearance of Jesus to an enemy or opponent of Christ. All the appearances were to those who were already believers. With a little thought, we can easily see why this was so, but nowhere in the Gospels are we told why it was so.

If the stories were made up, they certainly would never had been made up in this way. If the Gospels are, as some would have us believe, fabrications constructed one hundred, two hundred, or three hundred years after the alleged events occurred, when all the people involved were dead and gone, Jesus would have been represented as appearing to Caiaphas, Annas, Pilate, and Herod, confounding them by His reappearance from the dead, but there is no suggestion of anything of this kind in the Gospel stories. Every appearance is to someone who is already a believer. Why is this so? This is so for the very evident reason that this was the way that things occurred. The Gospel narratives are not concerned with producing a story for effect, but simply with recording events precisely as they occurred and as they were observed.

We find still another example in the fact that the

recorded appearances of Jesus after His resurrection were only occasional. He would appear in the midst of His disciples and then disappear, not being seen again for several days. We can easily understand why this was so. Jesus was trying to wean His disciples from their old-time communion with Him in the body and to prepare them for the communion in the Spirit of the days that were to come.

We are not, however, told this in the Gospel narrative. We are left to discover it for ourselves. It is doubtful if the disciples themselves at the time realized the meaning of the facts. If they had been making up a story to produce effect, they would have represented Jesus as being with them constantly, as living with them and eating and drinking with them day after day. Why, then, is the story told as recorded in the four Gospels? It is because this is the way that it had all occurred, and the Gospel writers were simply concerned with giving an exact representation of the facts as witnessed by themselves and by others.

We find another very remarkable example in what is recorded concerning the words of Jesus to Mary at their first meeting. In John 20:17, Jesus is recorded as saying to Mary, *Touch Me not, for I am not yet ascended to My Father.* We are not told why Jesus said this to Mary. We are left to discover the reason for ourselves if we can. The commentators have had a great deal of trouble trying to learn the reason for this. They vary widely from one another in their explanations of the words of Jesus. Go to the commentaries and you will find that one commentary gives one reason, and another commentary gives a different reason, and so on.

I have a reason of my own that I have never seen in any commentary, and I am convinced that it is the true reason, but I have never been able to convince others that it was the true reason. Why, then, was this little utterance of Jesus put in the Gospel record without a word of explanation, and which it has taken twenty centuries to explain, yet it is not yet completely and satisfactorily explained?

Certainly a writer making up a story would not put a little detail like that in it without any apparent meaning and without any attempt to explain it. Stories that are made up are made up for a purpose. Details that are inserted are inserted for a purpose, a purpose that is more or less evident. However, twenty centuries of study have not been able to find out the purpose for why this was inserted. Why, then, is it there? It is there because this is exactly what happened. This is what Jesus said. This is what Mary heard. This is what Mary told. Therefore, this is what John recorded. We do not have fiction here, but an accurate record of words spoken by Jesus after His resurrection.

We do not have fiction here, but an accurate record of words spoken by Jesus after His resurrection.

Another incidental detail that is introduced in the Gospel narrative and that is decisive proof of its historical accuracy is found in John 19:34. We are told that when one of the soldiers pierced the side of our crucified Lord with a spear, blood and water immediately came out, but we are not told the reason for this. In fact, the writer could not have known the reason.

There was no one on earth at the time who had sufficient knowledge of physiology to have known the reason. It was only centuries later that the physiological reason was discovered. The distinguished medical authority, Dr. Simpson of Edinburgh University, the discoverer of chloroform, wrote a powerful brochure during his lifetime in which he showed on scientific grounds that Jesus Christ died from what is called in scientific language "extravasation of the blood," or in popular language, "a broken heart."

When one dies in this way, the arms are thrown out (of course, Jesus' arms were already stretched out on the cross), and there is a loud cry (such as Jesus uttered, *My God, My God, why hast Thou forsaken Me?*). "The blood escapes into the pericardium and prevents the heart from beating. There the blood stands for a short time; it separates into serum (the water) and clot (the red corpuscles, blood). When the soldier pierced the bag (pericardium), the blood and water flowed out." This is the scientific explanation of the recorded fact, but John did not know this explanation. No one then living knew it, and no one knew it for centuries afterward.

Is it conceivable that a writer who made up an account of events that never occurred would have made up and inserted a fact that has a strict scientific explanation, fitting precisely into the various facts recorded, but an explanation that neither he nor anyone living at the time could possibly have known? How, then, did it come to be recorded in this way? It was because this is precisely what occurred, and although John did not know the explanation, he observed the fact and recorded the fact as observed, leaving it for time and scientific discovery to conclusively demonstrate the historical accuracy of what he told.

Beyond a doubt, we do not have any fiction here, but an exact record of something that occurred and was observed precisely as recorded. In the next chapter I will give you many more examples and more remarkable illustrations of the self-evident and unquestionable truthfulness of the Gospel accounts of the resurrection of Christ.

Chapter 6

The Self-Evident Truthfulness
of the Gospel Stories
of the Resurrection

In the previous chapter, we began the consideration of the question, "Did Jesus really rise from the dead?" We started out without assuming anything whatever. We started with the well-known fact that we have the four Gospels. Whether true or false, and whoever may have written them, we certainly have them. We laid these four Gospels side by side and tried to discover from the study of them whether they were the record of events that actually occurred, or whether they were fiction. We saw that it often happens that when an eye-witness is on the stand that the unintentional evidence he bears by words, phrases, and incidental details is more effective than his direct testimony because it is not the testimony of the witness, but the testimony of the truth to itself. We gave some examples of this, and in this chapter we will give some more.

Turn to John 20:24-25: *But Thomas, one of the twelve, called Didymus, was not with them when Jesus came. The other disciples therefore said unto him, We have seen the Lord. But he said unto them, Except I shall see in His hands the print of the nails, and put my finger into the print of the nails, and thrust my hand into His side, I will not believe.*

How true this all is to life! It is in perfect harmony with what is told to us about Thomas elsewhere. Thomas was the doubter in the apostolic company, the man who seems to have been governed by the testimony of his senses. Thomas is the one who, when Jesus said that He was going again into Judea, despondently said, *Let us also go that we may die with Him* (John 11:15-16). It was Thomas who, in John 14:4-5, when Jesus said, *Whither I go ye know the way*, replied, *Lord, we know not whither Thou goest, and how can we know the way?* It is Thomas who now says, *Except I shall see in His hands the print of the nails, and put my finger into the print of the nails, and thrust my hand into His side, I will not believe.* Is this made up, or is it life? To make it up would require literary talent that immeasurably exceeded the possibilities of the author.

Look now at John 20:4-6: *So they ran both together: and the other disciple did outrun Peter, and came first to the sepulcher. And he, stooping down and looking in, saw the linen clothes lying; yet went he not in. Then cometh Simon Peter following him, and went into the sepulcher.*

This again is quite consistent with what we know

of the men. Mary, returning hurriedly from the tomb, burst in upon the two disciples, and exclaimed, *They have taken away the Lord out of the sepulcher, and we know not where they have laid Him* (John 20:2). John and Peter jumped to their feet and ran to the tomb as quickly as they could. John was the younger of the two disciples. We are not told this in the narrative, but we learn it from other sources. Being younger, he was faster. He out-ran Peter and reached the tomb first. However, being a man of reserved and reverent disposition, he did not enter the tomb, but simply stooped down and looked in.

> Here again we have the unmistakable marks of truth and life.

Then Peter came along behind as fast as he could, but when he reached the tomb, he did not wait a moment outside, but plunged right in. Is this made up, or is it life? The person would indeed be a literary artist of incredible ability who had the skill to make this up if it did not happen just as we were told. Incidentally, there is also a touch of local accuracy in the report. When one visits the tomb today that scholars now accept as the real burial place of Christ, he will find himself unconsciously required to stoop down to look in.

Now turn to John 21:7: *Therefore that disciple whom Jesus loved saith unto Peter, It is the Lord. Now when Simon Peter heard that it was the Lord, he girt his fisher's coat unto him (for he was naked), and did cast himself into the sea.* Here again we have the unmistakable marks of truth and life. Recall the circumstances.

The apostles went at Jesus' commandment into

Galilee to meet Him there. Jesus did not immediately appear. Simon Peter, with the fisherman's passion still strong in his heart, said that he was going fishing. The others said that they would go with him. They fished all night and caught nothing. In the early dawn, Jesus stood upon the shore, but the disciples did not recognize Him in the dim light. Jesus asked them if they had anything to eat, and they answered, "No."

He urged them to cast their net on the right side of the boat to catch the fish. When the cast was made, they were not able to draw it in because of the multitude of fish. In an instant, John, the man of quick spiritual perception, said, *It is the Lord.* No sooner did Peter, a man of more-impulsive action, hear this, than he grabbed his fisherman's coat, threw it around him, threw himself overboard, and started swimming for shore to reach the Lord.

Is this made up, or is it life? This is no fiction. If some unknown author of the fourth Gospel made this up, he would be the master literary artist of the ages. We should take down every other name from the literary pantheon and place his name above them all.

Here is another example. Read John 20:15: *Jesus saith unto her, Woman, why weepest thou? Whom seekest thou? She, supposing Him to be the gardener, saith unto Him, Sir, if thou have borne Him hence, tell me where thou have laid Him, and I will take Him away.* This is surely a touch that surpasses the talent of anyone of that day, or any day.

Mary had gone into the city and notified Peter and John that she had found the sepulcher empty. They started running toward the sepulcher. Since Mary had already made the journey twice, they easily outran her, but wearily and slowly she made her way back to the tomb. Peter and John were long gone by the time she reached it. Brokenhearted and thinking that the tomb of her beloved Lord had been desecrated, she stood outside the tomb weeping.

Two angels were sitting in the tomb, one at the head and the other at the feet where the body of Jesus had lain, but the grief-stricken woman had no eye for angels. They said unto her, *Woman, why weepest thou?* She replied, *Because they have taken away my Lord, and I know not where they have laid Him.* She heard footsteps in the leaves behind her, and she turned around to see who was coming. She saw Jesus standing there, but blinded by tears and despair, she did not recognize her Lord.

Jesus said to her, *Why weepest thou? Whom seekest thou?* She thought it was the gardener who was talking to her, and she answered, *Sir, if thou have borne Him hence, tell me where thou hast laid Him, and I will take Him away.* Remember who it is who made the offer and what she offered to do. A weak woman offered to carry away a fully grown man. Of course she could not do it, but how true it is to a woman's nature that always forgets its weakness and never stops at impossibilities. There is something to be done, and she says, "I will do it." *Tell me where thou hast laid Him, and I will take Him away.* Is this made up? Never! This is life! This is reality! This is truth!

We see another example in Mark 16:7: *But go your way, tell His disciples and Peter that He goeth before you into Galilee: there shall ye see Him, as He said unto you.* I want you to notice two words: *and Peter.* Why *and Peter*? Wasn't Peter one of the disciples? He certainly was. He was at the head of the apostolic company. Why, then, was it said, *Tell His disciples and Peter*?

No explanation is given in the text, but reflection shows that it was an utterance of love toward the disheartened, despairing disciple who had three times denied his Lord. If the message had simply been to the disciples, Peter would have said, "Yes, I was once a disciple, but I can no longer be considered to be one. I denied my Lord three times on that dreadful night with oaths and cursing. It doesn't mean me."

However, our tender, compassionate Lord, through His angelic messengers, sent the message, "Go and tell His disciples, and whoever you tell, be sure you tell poor, weak, faltering, brokenhearted Peter." Is this made up, or is this a real picture of our Lord? I pity the person who is so undiscerning that he can think this is fiction.

Incidentally, let it be noticed that this is recorded only in the Gospel of Mark, which, as is well known, is Peter's Gospel. As Peter dictated to Mark what he should record, I can imagine Peter turning to Mark with tearful eyes and a grateful heart, saying, "Mark, be sure you put that in: *Tell His disciples and Peter!*"

Turn now to John 20:27-29: *Then saith He to Thomas, Reach hither thy finger, and behold My hands; and reach hither thy hand, and thrust it into My side: and be not faithless, but believing. And Thomas answered and said unto Him, My Lord and my God. Jesus saith unto him,*

Thomas, because thou hast seen Me, thou hast believed: blessed are they that have not seen, and yet have believed.

Notice both the action of Thomas and the rebuke of Jesus. Each is too characteristic to be attributed to the art of some master of fiction. Thomas had not been with the disciples at the first appearance of our Lord. A week had passed by, and another Lord's Day had come. This time, Thomas made sure he was present. If the Lord was going to appear, Thomas was going to be there. If he had been like some modern skeptics, he would have made an effort to be away, but even though he was a doubter, he was an honest doubter, and he wanted to know. Suddenly Jesus stood in the midst. He said to Thomas, *Reach hither thy finger, and behold My hands; and reach hither thy hand, and thrust it into My side: and be not faithless, but believing.* Thomas' eyes were opened at last. His faith, long held back, burst every barrier and carried Thomas to a higher height than any other disciple had yet gone. Exultingly and adoringly, he looked up into the face of Jesus and said, *My Lord and my God.*

Then Jesus tenderly, but searchingly, rebuked him. *Thomas,* He said, *because thou hast seen Me, thou hast believed: blessed are they* (who are so eager to find, so quick to see, and so ready to accept the truth that they do not wait for a visual demonstration, but are ready to take truth on adequate testimony) *that have not seen, and yet have believed.* Is this made up, or is this life? Is this a record of facts as they occurred, or is it a fictitious production of some master artist?

Turn now to John 21:21-22: *Peter seeing him saith to*

Jesus, Lord, and what shall this man do? Jesus saith unto him, If I will that he tarry till I come, what is that to thee? Follow thou Me. Let us see the context of these words. The disciples were on the beach of Galilee. Breakfast was over, and Jesus had told Peter that he was going to glorify Him in a martyr's death. Jesus then started to walk down the beach, and He said to Peter, *Follow Me.* Peter began to follow, but then he looked back over his shoulder to see what the others were doing. He saw John following too. With characteristic curiosity, Peter said, *Lord, if I am to die for Thee, what shall this man do?*

Jesus never answered questions of mere speculative curiosity regarding others, but He pointed the questioner to his own duty. On another occasion (Luke 13:23-24), someone went to Jesus and asked, *Are there few who will be saved?* Jesus replied to the question by telling them to make sure that they were saved themselves.

Now He points curious Peter away from questions that do not concern him regarding others and points to Peter's own immediate duty. Jesus said, *If I will that he tarry till I come, what is that to thee? Follow thou Me.* Is this made up, or is this life and reality?

Turn to other verses in the same chapter, John 21:15-17:

> *So when they had dined, Jesus saith to Simon Peter, Simon, son of Jonas, lovest thou Me more than these? He saith unto Him, Yea, Lord; Thou knowest that I love Thee. He saith unto him, Feed My lambs. He saith to him again the second time, Simon, son of Jonas, lovest thou Me? He*

> *saith unto Him, Yea, Lord; Thou knowest*
> *that I love Thee. He saith unto him, Feed*
> *My sheep. He saith unto him the third time,*
> *Simon, son of Jonas, lovest thou Me? Peter*
> *was grieved because He said unto him the*
> *third time, Lovest thou Me? And he said*
> *unto Him, Lord, Thou knowest all things;*
> *Thou knowest that I love Thee. Jesus saith*
> *unto him, Feed My sheep.*

What I want you to especially notice here are the words, *Peter was grieved because He said unto him the third time, Lovest thou Me?* Why did Jesus ask Peter three times, *Lovest thou Me?*

Why was Peter grieved because Jesus asked him three times? We are not told in the text, but if we read it in the light of Peter's thrice-repeated, threefold denial of His Lord, we will understand

No, this is not fiction; this is simply reporting what actually occurred.

it. Peter had denied the Lord three times, and Jesus gave Peter an opportunity to reaffirm his love three times. As tender as this was, it also reminded Peter of that terrible night when he had denied the Lord three times in the courtyard of Annas and Caiaphas. Peter was grieved because He said unto him the third time, *Lovest thou Me?*

Is this made up? Did the writer make it up with this fact in view? If he did, he surely would have mentioned it. No, this is not fiction; this is simply reporting what actually occurred. The accurate truthfulness of the record comes out even more strikingly in the Greek than in the English translation. Two different words are used for love. Jesus, in asking Peter, *Lovest thou Me?* used a strong word of a higher form of love. When Peter replied, *Lord, Thou knowest I love Thee,* he used a weaker word, but a more tender word (I am fond of You). The second time, Jesus used the stronger word, *Lovest thou Me?* and Peter replied the second time using the weaker word. In His third question, Jesus came down to Peter's level and used the weaker word that Peter had used. Peter replied, Lord, *Thou knowest all things; Thou knowest that I love Thee,* using the same weaker word.

Notice again the appropriateness of the way in which Jesus revealed Himself to different people after His resurrection. To Mary, He simply revealed Himself by calling her by name. Read John 20:16: *Jesus saith unto her, Mary. She turned herself, and saith unto Him, Rabboni; which is to say, Master.* What a delicate touch of nature we have here! Mary, as we saw a few moments ago, was standing outside the tomb overcome with grief. She had not recognized her Lord, even though He had spoken to her. She had mistaken Him for the gardener. She said, *Sir, if thou hast borne Him hence, tell me where thou hast laid Him, and I will take Him away.*

Then Jesus uttered just one word. He said, *Mary.* As that name came trembling on the morning air, uttered with the old familiar tone and spoken as no one else had ever spoken it but He, her eyes were opened in an instant. She fell at His feet and tried to hold on to them. She looked up into His face and cried, *Rabboni; my Master.*

Is that made up? No. This is life. This is Jesus, and this is the woman who loved Him. No unknown author of the second, third, or fourth century has produced such a masterpiece as this. We stand here unquestionably face to face with reality, with life, and with Jesus and Mary as they actually were.

Jesus made Himself known to the two men who were on the road to Emmaus in the breaking of bread. Read Luke 24:30-31: *And it came to pass, as He sat at meat with them, He took bread, and blessed it, and brake, and gave to them. And their eyes were opened, and they knew Him: and He vanished out of their sight.*

They knew Him in the breaking of bread. Why? The evangelist gives no explanation, but it is not hard to read between the lines and find the explanation. In each one of the Gospels, emphatic mention is made of Jesus giving thanks at meals. There was something so characteristic in the way He gave thanks at meals that was so real, so different, from the way in which they had ever seen anyone else do it. There was such an evident approach into the very presence of God that was so utterly unlike the formality and unreality of others at such a time, that the moment Jesus lifted up His eyes and gave thanks, their eyes were opened and they knew Him. This, too, is reality and life, and not fiction.

To Thomas, the man governed by his senses, Jesus made Himself known by showing the very print of the nails in His hands and the hole in His side. To John and

Peter, He made Himself known as at the beginning in the miraculous catch of fish. Everywhere, in each specific detail, the narrative has a consistency and a truth to life that makes the supposition of fiction impossible.

Look at one more example. Carefully read John 20:7: *And the napkin that was about His head, not lying with the linen clothes, but wrapped together in a place by itself.* How strange that such a little detail as this would be added to the story with absolutely no attempt of saying why, yet how deeply significant this little unexplained detail is!

When I was studying in the theological seminary, an upperclassman came home one Sunday afternoon from his Bible class quite disgusted. He taught a class of young working women about twenty years of age. He said, "One of my scholars asked me a stupid question today. She asked me if there was any significance in the napkin being wrapped together in a place by itself. As if there was any significance in that!" In reality, though, it was not a stupid working girl, but a stupid theologian, for there is indeed the deepest significance in the napkin being folded and placed by itself.

Jesus Christ was dead. For three days and three nights, from Wednesday evening at sunset until Saturday evening at sunset, His body lay cold and silent in the sepulcher, as truly dead as anybody was ever dead, but at last the appointed hour came. The breath of God swept through the sleeping and silent clay, and in that supreme moment of His own earthly life, that supreme moment of human history, when Jesus rose triumphant over death and Satan, there was no excitement upon

His part. With that same faith and trust in the Father's abiding care that characterized His whole career, with the same calm that He displayed upon storm-tossed Galilee when His frightened disciples shook Him from His sleep and said, *Lord, carest Thou not that we perish*, and He arose on the deck of the tossing vessel and said to the raging waves and winds, *Be still!* and there was a great calm, so now again in this glorious, this wonderful moment, He did not excitedly tear the napkin from His face and throw it aside, but absolutely without human haste or commotion or disorder, He took it calmly from His head, rolled it up, and laid it away in an orderly manner by itself.

Was that made up? Never! Never! This is not a delicate masterpiece of the romance novelist's art. We read here the simple narrative of a matchless detail in a unique life that was actually lived here upon earth, a life so exquisitely beautiful that one cannot read it with an honest and open mind without feeling the tears coming to his eyes.

> It is in just such little things that the fiction would disclose itself.

Someone will say, "These are little things." True, but it is from that very fact that they gain very much of their significance. It is in just such little things that the fiction would disclose itself. Fiction displays its difference from fact in the little things. In the great outstanding plots you can make fiction look like truth, but when you come to examine it closely and microscopically, you will soon detect that it is not reality, but fabrication. However, the more microscopically we examine the Gospel narratives, the more we become impressed with their truthfulness. The genuineness, naturalness, and self-evident truthfulness of the narratives down to the smallest detail surpass all the possibilities of deceit.

Chapter 7

The Circumstantial Evidence of the Resurrection of Christ

In the last two chapters, we have been considering some of the internal proofs of the truthfulness of the Gospel story. In this chapter we consider the circumstantial evidence for the resurrection of Christ. I suppose you know what is meant by circumstantial evidence.

Circumstantial evidence refers to certain proven or admitted facts or circumstances that demand for their explanation of the other fact that we are seeking to prove. For example, a man was once found murdered. The only clue to the murderer was the point of a knife blade that was found broken off in the heart. With this clue, the detectives went to work.

A knife was found with a broken blade. The jagged edges of the broken blade fit exactly into the notches in the point that had been found in the heart. Moreover, there were traces of blood upon both point and blade, and the traces of blood on the point exactly fit the traces of blood on the blade. It was considered to be proven that the murder was committed with that knife.

Take another illustration. A bolt of cloth was stolen from a certain manufacturer. A search was made for the bolt of cloth. A bolt of cloth was found that the manufacturer claimed was his stolen bolt. However, the man in whose possession the bolt was found claimed that the bolt came from an entirely different factory. When the bolt of cloth was taken to the factory from which the bolt had been stolen, the holes at each end of the bolt of cloth fit exactly upon the frame at the factory from which it was alleged to have been stolen, but when it was taken to the factory from which the man claimed to have obtained it, it was found that the holes in the end of the bolt of cloth did not at all fit upon the frame of that factory. On this evidence it was considered to be proven that the bolt of cloth had come from the factory where it fitted upon the frame.

There is abundant evidence of this kind as to the certainty of the resurrection of Christ from the dead. There are certain proven and admitted facts that demand the resurrection of Christ to account for them.

1. Beyond a question, the foundational truth preached in the early years of the church's history was the resurrection. This was the one doctrine that the apostles were always proclaiming. Whether or not Jesus actually rose from the dead, it is certain that the one thing that the apostles constantly proclaimed was that He had risen.

Why would the apostles use this as the very corner-stone of their creed if it was not well attested and firmly believed? Furthermore, they laid down their lives for this doctrine. People do not lay down their lives for a doctrine that they do not firmly believe. They stated that they had seen Jesus after His resurrection, and rather than give up their statement, they died for it.

Of course, people can die for error, and they often have. However, in this case they would know whether or not they had seen Jesus, and they would not merely have been dying for error, but would be dying for a statement that they knew to be false. This is not credible.

> People do not lay down their lives for a doctrine that they do not firmly believe.

Furthermore, if the apostles really firmly believed, as is admitted, that Jesus rose from the dead, they had some facts upon which they founded their belief. These are the facts they would have related in recounting the story, and they would not have made up a story out of imaginary incidents. However, if the facts were as recounted in the Gospels, there is no possibility of escaping the conclusion that Jesus actually arose.

Also, if Jesus had not arisen, there would have been some evidence that He had not arisen. His enemies would have found this evidence, but the apostles went up and down the very city where He had been cruci-fied and proclaimed right to the face of the murderers that He had been raised, and no one could produce evidence to the contrary. The best they could do was to say that the guards fell asleep and the disciples stole the body while the guards slept (Matthew 28:12-15). People who bear evidence to what happens while they are asleep are hardly credible witnesses. Even more, if the apostles had stolen the body, they would have known it themselves, and would not have been ready to die for what they knew to be a fraud.

2. Another known fact is the change in the day of rest. The early church came from among the Jews. From time immemorial, the Jews had celebrated the seventh day of the week as their day of rest and worship, but we find the early Christians in the Acts of the Apostles, and also in early Christian writings, assembling on the first day of the week.

There is nothing more difficult than to change a holy day that has been celebrated for centuries and that is one of the most cherished customs of the people. What is especially significant about the change is that it was changed by no clear decree, but by general consent. Something tremendous must have happened that led to this change. The apostles asserted that what had happened on that day was the resurrection of Christ from the dead, and that is the most rational explanation. In fact, it is the only reasonable explanation for the change.

3. The most significant fact of all is the change, the moral transformation, in the disciples. At the time of Christ's crucifixion, we find the whole apostolic company filled with blank and utter despair. We see Peter,

the leader of the apostolic company, denying his Lord three times with oaths and cursing.

A few days later, though, we see this same man filled with a courage that nothing could shake. We see Peter standing before the very council that had condemned Jesus to death, and saying to them, *Be it known unto you all, and to all the people of Israel, that in the name of Jesus of Nazareth, whom ye crucified, whom God raised from the dead, doth this man stand before you whole* (Acts 4:10). A little later, when commanded by this council not to speak at all nor teach in the name of Jesus, we hear Peter and John answering, *Whether it be right in the sight of God to hearken unto you more than unto God, judge ye. For we cannot but speak the things which we have seen and heard* (Acts 4:19-20).

A little later still, after being arrested and imprisoned and in peril of death, when sternly arraigned by the council, we hear Peter and the other apostles answering their demand that they should be silent regarding Jesus. They answered, *We ought to obey God rather than man. The God of our Fathers raised up Jesus whom ye slew and hanged on a tree. Him hath God exalted with His right hand to be a Prince and a Saviour, and we are His witnesses of these things* (Acts 5:29-32).

Something tremendous must have happened to account for such a radical and astounding moral transformation as this. Nothing short of the fact of the resurrection, of their having seen the risen Lord, will explain it.

These unquestionable facts are so impressive and so conclusive that even atheistic and Jewish scholars now admit that the apostles believed that Jesus rose from the dead. Even Ferdinand Baur admits this. Even David Strauss says, "Only this much need be acknowledged, that the apostles firmly believed that Jesus had arisen." Strauss evidently does not want to admit any more than he has to, but he feels compelled to admit this much. Schenkel goes further yet and says, "It is an indisputable fact that in the early morning of the first day of the week following the crucifixion, the grave of Jesus was found empty. It is a second fact that the disciples and other members of the apostolic communion were convinced that Jesus was seen after the crucifixion." These admissions are fatal to the rationalists who make them.

The question at once arises as to where this conviction and belief come from. Ernest Renan, in his book *The Life of Jesus*, attempts an answer by saying that "the passion of a hallucinated woman (Mary) gives to the world a resurrected God." By this, Renan means that Mary was in love with Jesus. After Jesus' crucifixion, Mary was grieving over it, and in the passion of her love, she dreamed herself into a condition where she had a hallucination that she had seen Jesus risen from the dead. She reported her dream as fact, and thus the passion of a hallucinated woman gave to the world a resurrected God.

However, we reply that the passion of a hallucinating woman was not competent to this task. Remember the makeup of the apostolic company. In the apostolic company were Matthew and Thomas, who needed to be convinced, and Saul was outside the group and needed to be converted. The passion of a hallucinating woman would not convince a stubborn unbeliever like Thomas or a Jewish tax collector like Matthew. Who ever heard of a tax collector who could be imposed upon by the passion of a hallucinating woman? Neither will the passion of a hallucinating woman convince a fierce and conscientious enemy like Saul of Tarsus. We must find some more reasonable explanation than this.

Strauss tried to account for it by inquiring whether the appearances might not have been visions. To this we reply that, first of all, there was no subjective starting point for such visions. The apostles, so far from expecting to see the Lord, hardly believed their own eyes when they did see Him. Furthermore, who ever heard of eleven men having the same vision at the same time, to say nothing of five hundred men having the same vision at the same time (1 Corinthians 15:6)? Strauss demands of us that we give up one miracle and substitute five hundred miracles in its place. Nothing can surpass the gullibility of unbelief.

> Nothing can surpass the gullibility of unbelief.

The third attempt at an explanation is that Jesus was not really dead when they took Him from the cross, that His friends worked over Him and brought Him back to life. They say that what was supposed to be the appearance of the risen Lord was the appearance of one who had never been really dead, but was only apparently dead, and was now merely resuscitated.

To sustain this view, argument has been made to the short time Jesus hung upon the cross and to the fact that history tells us of one in the time of Josephus who had been taken down from the cross and nursed back to life. However, we answer to this first that we must remember the events that preceded the crucifixion – the agony in the garden of Gethsemane, the awful ordeal of the four trials, the scourging, and the consequent physical condition in which all this left Jesus. Remember, too, the water and the blood that poured from the pierced side.

In the second place, we reply that His enemies would have taken, and did take, all necessary precautions against such a thing as this happening (John 19:34). Third, we reply that if Jesus had been merely resuscitated, He would have been so weak and would have been such an utter physical wreck that His reappearance would have been measured at its real value, and the moral transformation in the disciples, for which we are trying to account, would still remain unaccounted for. The officer in the time of Josephus who is cited in proof, though he was brought back to life, was an utter physical wreck.

We reply, in the fourth place, that if Jesus had merely been brought back to life, the apostles and friends of Jesus, who are the ones who are supposed to have brought Him back to life, would have known how they brought Him back to life. They would have known that it was not a case of resurrection but of resuscitation, and the main fact to be accounted for, the change in themselves, would remain unaccounted for. The attempted explanation is an explanation that does not explain.

Fifth, we reply that the moral difficulty is the

greatest of all. If it was merely a case of resuscitation, then Jesus tried to pass Himself off as one risen from the dead, when He was nothing of the sort. That would make Him a great impostor, and the whole Christian system would rest on fraud as its ultimate foundation. Is it possible to believe that such a system of religion as that of Jesus Christ, embodying such exalted precepts and principles of truth, purity, and love, began with a deliberately planned fraud? No one whose own heart is not polluted by fraud and deceit can believe that Jesus was an impostor and that His religion was founded upon fraud.

We have eliminated all other possible suppositions. Only one remains – that Jesus really was raised from the dead on the third day as is recorded in the Gospels. The desperate straits to which those who attempt to deny it are driven are themselves proof of the fact.

We also have several independent lines of argument that point decisively to the resurrection of Christ from the dead. Some of these taken separately prove the fact, but taken together they constitute an argument that makes doubt of the resurrection of Christ impossible to the honest person.

Of course, if someone is determined not to believe, no amount of proof will convince him. Such a person must be left to his own deliberate choice of error and falsehood, but anyone who really desires to know the truth and is willing to obey it at any cost must accept the resurrection of Christ as a historically proven fact.

There is really only one serious objection to the doctrine that Christ arose from the dead, and that is that there is no conclusive evidence that anyone else ever arose from the dead. A sufficient answer to this would be that even if it were certain that no one else ever arose, it would not at all prove that Jesus did not rise, for the life of Jesus was unique. His nature was unique, His character was unique, His mission was unique, and His history was unique, and it is not to be wondered at, but is rather to be expected, that the end of such a life would also be unique.

After all, this objection is simply David Hume's exploded argument against the possibility of the miraculous revamped. According to this argument, no amount of evidence can prove a miracle because miracles are contrary to all experience. But are miracles contrary to all experience? To start out by saying this is to beg the very question at issue. They may be outside of your experience and mine, and they may be outside the experience of this entire generation, but your experience and mine and the experience of this entire generation is not all experience.

Every student of geology and astronomy knows that things have occurred in the past that are entirely outside the experience of the present generation. Things have occurred within the last four years that are entirely outside the experience of the previous fifty years. True science does not start out with an *a priori* hypothesis that certain things are impossible. It simply studies the evidence to know what has actually occurred. It does not twist its observed facts to make them harmonize with *a priori* theories, but it seeks to make its theories harmonize with facts as observed.

To say that miracles are impossible and that no amount of evidence can therefore prove a miracle is to be incredibly unscientific. Within the past few years in the realm of chemistry, for example, discoveries have been made regarding radium that seemed to run counter to all previous observations regarding chemical elements and to well-established chemical theories, but the scientist has not therefore said that these discoveries about radium cannot be true. Instead, he has gone to work to find out where the trouble was in his previous theories. The observed and recorded facts in the case before us prove that Jesus rose from the dead, and true science must accept that conclusion and conform its theories to this observed fact.

> The observed and recorded facts in the case before us prove that Jesus rose from the dead, and true science must accept that conclusion and conform its theories to this observed fact.

In the day of the great triumph of deism in England, two of the most brilliant men in the denial of the supernatural were the eminent legal authorities Gilbert West and Lord Lyttelton. These two men, who were put forward to crush the defenders of the supernatural in the Bible, had a conference together. One of them said to the other that it would be difficult to maintain their position unless they disposed of two of the alleged bulwarks of Christianity – the alleged resurrection of Jesus from the dead and the alleged conversion of Saul of Tarsus.

Lyttelton agreed to write a book to show that Saul of

Tarsus was never converted as is recorded in the Acts of the Apostles, but that his alleged conversion was a myth, if Gilbert West would write another book to show that the alleged resurrection of Christ from the dead was a myth. West said to Lyttelton, "I will have to depend upon you for my facts, for I am somewhat rusty in the Bible," to which Lyttelton replied that he was counting upon West, for he, too, was somewhat rusty in the Bible. One of them said to the other, "If we are to be honest in the matter, we ought to at least study the evidence," and this they set out to do.

They met together numerous times while they were preparing their works. In one of these conferences, West said to Lyttelton that there had been something on his mind for some time that he thought he ought to speak to him about, that as he had been studying the evidence, he was beginning to feel that there was something in it. Lyttelton replied that he was glad that he had spoken about it in this way, for he himself was somewhat shaken, as he had been studying the evidence for the conversion of Saul of Tarsus.

Finally, when the books were finished, the two men met. West said to Lyttelton, "Have you written your book?" He replied that he had, but he said, "West, as I have been studying the evidence and weighing it by the recognized laws of legal evidence, I have become satisfied that Saul of Tarsus was converted as is stated in the Acts of the Apostles, and that Christianity is true, and I have written my book on that side." The book can be found today in first-class libraries.

"Well," said West, "as I have studied the evidence

for the resurrection of Jesus Christ from the dead, and have weighed it according to the acknowledged laws of evidence, I have become satisfied that Jesus really rose from the dead as recorded in the Gospels, and I have written my book on that side." This book also can be found in our libraries today.

Let anyone of legal mind, anyone who is accustomed and competent to weigh evidence, yes, anyone with fair reasoning powers, and, above all, with complete honesty, sit down to study the facts regarding the resurrection of Jesus Christ from the dead, and he will become satisfied that beyond any doubt Jesus rose from the dead as is recorded in the Gospels. Suppose Jesus did rise from the dead? What then? We will take that question up in the next chapter.

Chapter 8

What the Resurrection of Jesus from the Dead Proves

I n our last three chapters, we have seen conclusive evidence that Jesus Christ rose from the dead. We have followed a number of independent lines of argument. Several of these taken alone satisfactorily prove the fact of the resurrection, but taken together they constitute an argument that makes doubt of the resurrection of Christ impossible to an honest mind.

However, what does it mean that He rose from the dead? What does His resurrection prove? It proves everything that most needs to be proved. It proves everything that is essential in Christianity.

First of all, the resurrection of Christ from the dead proves that there is a God, and that the God of the Bible is the true God. Every effect must have an adequate cause, and the only adequate cause that will account for the resurrection of Jesus Christ is God, the God of the Bible.

When Jesus was here upon earth, He proclaimed the God of the Bible to be the God of Abraham, Isaac, and Jacob (Matthew 22:32-34), the God of the Old Testament as well as the New. He claimed that after He would be put to death, the God of Abraham, Isaac, and Jacob, the God of the Bible, would raise Him from the dead on the third day.

This was an astonishing claim to make, and humanly, it was an absurd claim. For centuries people had come and gone. They had lived and died, and as far as human observation went, that was the end of them. Jesus, though, claimed that after all these centuries of people living, dying, and passing into oblivion, that God, the God of the Bible, would raise Him from the dead.

Jesus died. He was crucified, He died, and He was buried. The appointed hour at which He had claimed God would raise Him from the dead came. God did indeed raise Him from the dead, and thereby Jesus' astounding claim was substantiated. It was decisively proven that there is a God and that the God of the Bible is the true God.

For centuries, people have been seeking for proof of the existence and character of God. There is the teleological argument, the argument from the marks of creative intelligence and design in the material universe. It is a good argument in its place. There is the argument from the intelligent guiding hand of God in human history. There is the ontological argument, and other arguments, all more or less convincing – but the resurrection of Jesus Christ from the dead provides us with a solid, scientific foundation for our faith in God.

In the light of the resurrection, our faith in God is built upon observed facts. In the light of the resurrection of Jesus, atheism and agnosticism no longer have any ground upon which to stand. Well might Peter say, *We through Him are believers in God, who raised Him from the dead, and gave Him glory* (1 Peter 1:21). My belief in the God of the Bible is not merely a charming imagination. It is a fixed faith resting upon an incontrovertibly firm fact.

> In the light of the resurrection, our faith in God is built upon observed facts.

In the second place, the resurrection of Jesus Christ from the dead proves that Jesus is a teacher sent from God who received His message from God, that He was absolutely inerrant, and that He spoke the very words of God.

This was Jesus' claim for Himself. In John 7:16, He says, *My teaching is not Mine, but His that sent Me.* In John 12:49, He says, *I have not spoken of Myself; but the Father which sent Me, He gave me a commandment, what I should say, and what I should speak.* In John 14:10-11, He says, *Believest thou not that I am in the Father, and the Father in Me? The words that I speak unto you I speak not of Myself: but the Father that dwelleth in Me, He doeth the works. Believe Me that I am in the Father, and the Father in Me: or else believe Me for the very works' sake.* In John 14:24, He says, *The word which ye hear is not Mine, but the Father's which sent Me.* His claim was that His words were the very words of God.

This, too, was an amazing claim to make. Others have made similar claims, but the difference between their claims and that of Jesus is that Jesus substantiated His claim, and no one else has ever substantiated his. God Himself unmistakably set His seal upon this astounding claim of Jesus Christ by raising Him from the dead. In the light of the resurrection of Jesus Christ from the dead, that school of criticism that assumes to question the absolute inerrancy of Jesus Christ as a teacher, and to set its authority up above that of Jesus, has absolutely no ground upon which to stand. Even more, by putting forward its unsubstantiated claims in opposition to the demonstrated claims of Jesus Christ, that school of criticism makes itself a laughingstock in the eyes of thoughtful people.

In the third place, the resurrection of Jesus Christ from the dead proves that He is the Son of God. The apostle Paul says in Romans 1:4 that Jesus is *declared to be the Son of God with power by the resurrection from the dead*, and anyone who will stop to think will see that this is true beyond any doubt.

When Jesus was here upon earth, He claimed to be divine in a sense in which no other man was divine. He taught that while even the greatest of God's prophets were only servants, He was a Son, an only Son (Mark 12:6, note the context). He claimed that He and the Father were one (John 10:30). He said that all people should honor Him, even as they honored the Father

(John 5:23). Jesus claimed that He was so completely and fully indwelt by God and was such a perfect and absolute incarnation of God that he who had seen Him had seen the Father (John 14:9).

This was a most amazing claim to make. This was a claim that, if not true, was outrageous blasphemy. Jesus told people that they would put Him to death for making this claim, but that after they had put Him to death, God Himself would set His seal to the claim by raising Him from the dead.

They did put Him to death for making this claim. The people of that day who did not believe in the deity of Jesus Christ caused Him to be nailed to the cross of Calvary for claiming to be divine (Matthew 26:63-66). However, when the appointed hour had come, the breath of God swept through the sleeping clay, and God Himself, as Jesus claimed He would, set His seal to Christ's assertion of His own deity by raising Him from the dead.

Thus God proclaimed to all ages, with a clearer voice than if He would speak from the open heavens today, "This is My only begotten Son, the One in whom I dwell in all My fullness, so that he who has seen Him has seen the Father." In the light of the resurrection of Jesus Christ from the dead, Unitarianism has absolutely no logical ground upon which to stand.

In the fourth place, the resurrection of Jesus Christ from the dead proves that there is a judgment day coming. On Mars Hill, Paul declared, *God hath appointed a day in which He will judge the world in righteousness* *by that Man whom He hath ordained, whereof He hath given assurance unto all men in that He hath raised Him from the dead* (Acts 17:31), thus making the resurrection of Christ the God-given assurance of the coming judgment.

How does the resurrection of Christ give assurance of coming judgment? When Jesus was upon earth, He declared that the Father had committed all judgment unto Him (John 5:22). He declared further that the hour was coming in which all who were in their graves would hear His voice and come forth. Those who had done good would come forth unto the resurrection of life, and those who had done evil unto the resurrection of judgment (John 5:28-29).

People ridiculed His claim, hated Him for making the claim, and put Him to death for making the claim and the other claim involved in it, that of deity, but God set His seal to the claim by raising Him from the dead. The resurrection of Jesus Christ from the dead, which is an absolutely certain fact of history in the past, points with an unerring finger to an absolutely certain coming judgment in the future.

Belief in a coming judgment day is not a mere guess of theologians. It is a positive faith founded upon a proven fact. In the light of the resurrection of Jesus Christ from the dead, the person who continues in sin, flattering himself with the hope that there will be no future day of reckoning and of judgment, is guilty of delusion. Jesus will sit in judgment, and every one of us must give account to Him for the deeds done in the body (2 Corinthians 5:10).

In the fifth place, the resurrection of Jesus Christ from the dead proves that every believer in Christ is justified from all things. We read in Romans 4:25 that Jesus *was delivered up for our trespasses, and was raised for our justification.* More literally, *He was delivered up because of our trespasses* (that is, because we had trespassed) *and was raised because of our justification* (that is, because we were justified).

The resurrection of Jesus Christ proves decisively that the believer in Him is justified. But how? When Jesus was on earth, He said that He would offer up His life a ransom for many (Matthew 20:28). The hour came, and He offered up His life on the cross of Calvary as a ransom for us. Now the atonement has been made, but there still remains a question: "Will God accept the atonement which has thus been offered?"

> The resurrection of Jesus Christ proves decisively that the believer in Him is justified.

For three nights and three days this question remained unanswered. Jesus was in the grave, cold and dead. The long-predicted hour came, the breath of God swept through that sleeping clay, and Christ rose triumphant from the dead. He was exalted to the right hand of the Father, and God proclaimed to the whole universe, "I have accepted the atonement that Jesus made."

When Jesus died, He died as my representative, and I died in Him. When He arose, He rose as my representative, and I arose in Him. When He ascended up on high and took His place at the right hand of the

Father in glory, He ascended as my representative, and I ascended in Him. Today I am seated in Christ with God in the heavenlies.

I look at the cross of Christ, and I know that atonement has been made for my sins. I look at the open sepulcher and the risen and ascended Lord, and I know that the atonement has been accepted. There no longer remains a single sin on me, no matter how many or how great my sins may have been. My sins may have been as high as the mountains, but in the light of the resurrection, the atonement that covers them is as high as heaven. My sins may have been as deep as the ocean, but in the light of the resurrection, the atonement that swallows them up is as deep as eternity. *Be it known unto you therefore, brethren, that through this Man is proclaimed unto you remission of sins, and by Him every one that believeth is justified from all things* (Acts 13:38-39).

In the sixth place, the resurrection of Jesus Christ from the dead proves that all who are united to Christ by a living faith will live again. Paul says, *If we believe that Jesus died and rose again, even so them also which sleep in Jesus will God bring with Him* (1 Thessalonians 4:14). The believer is so united to Christ by a living faith that if Christ rose, we must also rise. If the grave could not hold Him, it cannot hold us.

For centuries, people have been seeking proof of immortality. We have had the dreams of poets and the speculations of philosophers to encourage us with the hope that we will live again, but the best philosophical arguments only point to the probability of a future life. In a matter like this, the human heart craves and demands something more than probability. In the resurrection of Jesus Christ from the dead, we get something more than probability. We get absolute certainty. We get scientific demonstration of life beyond the grave. The resurrection of Jesus Christ removes the hope of immortality from the domain of the speculative and the probable and places it into the domain of the scientifically demonstrated and certain. We know there is life beyond the grave.

A popular preacher has recently said, "Not a few are not at all sure that there is any life beyond the grave. They wish it could be proven. So do I. But we can do no more than infer it from the moral constitution of the universe." Thank God that this popular preacher is wrong. Before the resurrection of Jesus Christ, perhaps we could "do no more than infer it from the moral constitution of the universe," but in the light of the resurrection, it is no longer left to uncertain inferences from the moral constitution of the universe; it is proven. No further proof is needed.

It is scientifically demonstrated, and to anyone who will honestly consider the facts regarding the resurrection of Christ, unbelief or agnosticism in regard to the future life becomes an impossibility. In the light of the first Easter morning, I go out into the cemeteries where the sleeping dust of father and mother, brother and child lie, and all my tears are brushed away, for I hear the Father saying, "Your father will live again.

Your mother will live again. Your brother will live again. Your child will live again."

In the seventh place, the resurrection of Jesus Christ from the dead proves that it is the privilege of believers to have daily, hourly, constant victory over sin. We are united not only to the Lord who died, and thus made atonement for our sin and delivered us from the guilt of sin, but we are also united to the Lord who rose again, who *ever liveth to make intercession for us* (Hebrews 7:25). We are united to the Lord who has power to save to the uttermost, power to keep us from falling day by day, and power to present us *faultless before the presence of His glory with exceeding joy* (Jude 24).

I may be weak, utterly weak, unable to resist temptation for a single hour, but He is strong, infinitely strong, and He lives to give me help and deliverance every day and every hour. The question of victory over sin is not a question of my weakness, but of His strength. His resurrection power is always at my disposal. He has all power in heaven and on earth, and what my risen Lord has belongs to me also. In the light of the resurrection of Jesus Christ from the dead, failure in daily living is unnecessary and inexcusable. In His resurrection life and power, it is our privilege and our duty to lead victorious lives.

Four men were once climbing up the slippery side of the Matterhorn. A guide and a tourist, a second guide and a second tourist, were all roped together. The lower tourist lost his footing and went over the side. The sudden pull on the rope carried the lower guide with him, and he carried the other tourist with him. Three men were then dangling over the dizzying cliff. However, the guide who was in the lead, feeling the first pull upon the rope, drove his pike into the ice, braced his feet, and held fast. Three men were dangling over the dreadful abyss, but the three men were safe because they were tied to the man who held fast. The first tourist regained his place upon the path, the guide regained his, and the lower tourist regained his, and on and up they went in safety.

As the human race ascended the icy cliffs of life, the first Adam lost his footing and was swept over the abyss. He pulled the next man after him, and the next, and the next, and the next, until the whole race hung over the abyss. However, the second Adam, Jesus Christ, stood fast, and all who are united to Him by a living faith, although dangling over the dreadful precipice, are safe, because they are tied to Christ.

Chapter 9

The Causes of Unbelief

The profession of unbelief is very common in our day. I am constantly meeting with those who give as their reason for not being Christians that they do not believe in the Bible. There are many preachers, most excellent and gifted men, who think that unbelief is not worthy of attention, that the proper way to treat it is to ignore it. I do not agree with them. Unbelief is common enough, active enough, and destructive enough to demand attention. While I do not for a moment think that the cause of Christ or the Bible has anything to fear from unbelief, I do know that individuals and communities are being greatly injured by it, and we owe it to them to expose its real character, to point out its consequences, and to show its cure. I have had no greater joy now for some years than to be able to lead many people out of the confusion and wretchedness of unbelief and into the clear light and abounding joy of an intelligent faith in Christ and the Bible.

Causes of Unbelief

What are the causes of unbelief?

The first cause, and one of the most common, is misrepresentation of Christianity by its professed disciples. There are two kinds of misrepresentations. There are misrepresentations in doctrine and misrepresentations in daily living.

Let us look first at the misrepresentations in doctrine. Take, for example, what has been preached as Christianity for generations in France, Spain, Italy, the Philippine Islands, Mexico, and the South American republics. Of course, we know that this is only a downright distortion of the Christianity of the Bible, but the common people of these lands do not know this. They suppose that the Christianity preached by the priests is the Christianity of the Bible. Is it any wonder that they reject it and become out-and-out atheists? If what is thus preached as Christianity were indeed Christianity, I can't help but think I would reject it myself.

However, many so-called Protestant representations of Christianity, if not just as false, are still false. There is a wide difference between the God of the Bible and the God of much of so-called Protestant teaching, between the Christ of the Bible and the Christ of much of so-called Protestant teaching, and between the Christian life as set forth in the Bible and the ethics set forth in the pulpit.

The most outrageous misrepresentations of Christianity on the part of its professed disciples are the misrepresentations in daily living. The lives of many professed Christians are so widely at variance with the life taught in the Bible that it leads many observers into absolute unbelief.

Take, for example, the professed Christian who oppresses his employees in their wages. How many professed Christian employers are there today who grind their employees almost beyond endurance? Is it any wonder that these employees say that they have no use for Christianity? Look at the professed Christians in business who are dishonest in trade, who misrepresent their merchandise, and who use all manner of dishonorable means to get ahead of their competitors in business. Is it any wonder that people looking on are led to give up such misrepresented Christianity?

The most outrageous misrepresentations of Christianity on the part of its professed disciples are the misrepresentations in daily living.

On one occasion, after the wedding of a young man in business in the city of Chicago, I began to speak to him about becoming a Christian. He replied, "You do not need to talk to me about that. I work for ----------------. These men are very prominent in the church, and we know how they carry on their business, as we work for them. I have no desire to be a Christian."

Look at the professed Christian who rolls up his millions and lives in lavish luxury while the poor are starving at his doors. You may say to me that these misrepresentations of Christianity are not a sufficient excuse for unbelief, that people should learn to distinguish between real Christianity and its counterfeit, and this I admit. Of course, a really intelligent person never refuses good money because there is counterfeit money in circulation, but many people do not distinguish between the two.

They do not read the Bible for themselves, and their only idea of Christianity is from what they see in the lives and teachings of its professed disciples. They say, "If that is Christianity, I do not want it," and so they become unbelievers. One of the most well-known unbelievers of modern times claimed that it was the inconsistent living of his own father, a Baptist preacher, that first led him into unbelief.

Whether his picture of his father's character was true or not, or whether to defend his own unbelief he greatly misrepresented his own father (as I have heard it said that he did), I cannot say, but I do know that beyond a question in many instances the inconsistencies of professedly Christian parents have led their children into absolute unbelief. Misrepresentation of Christianity by its professed disciples in their teachings, and especially in their lives, has done more to produce atheists than all the writings and speeches that all the Paines and Voltaires and Ingersolls ever gave to the world.

The second cause of unbelief is ignorance: ignorance of what the Bible contains and teaches, ignorance of history, and ignorance of true science. The average unbeliever knows almost nothing about the Bible. He has heard about a few difficulties here and there from the writings or speeches of other atheists, but he knows practically nothing about the actual contents of the Bible.

I once asked a man if he would become a Christian. He replied, "No, I do not believe the Bible."

"Why don't you believe the Bible?"

"Because the Bible is so full of contradictions."

"Well," I said, "if the Bible is full of contradictions, please show me one."

"It is full of them."

"If it is full of them, you should be able to show me at least one."

"Well, it is full of them."

"Then show me one."

"Well, it is in the book of Psalms."

I handed my Bible to him so he could find it, and he began looking for the Psalms in the back part of the New Testament. "Let me find the book of Psalms for you."

After I found the book of Psalms for him, he began to fumble around for a while, and then he said, "If I had my Bible here, I could show it to you."

I asked, "Will you bring your Bible tonight and meet me here at the close of the meeting?" He promised that he would. The appointed hour came, and I was at the appointed place, but my unbelieving friend did not appear. I had taken the precaution of asking him for his address, and I went to the address he had given. It was a tavern, but I did not find the man. Months later, after one of our meetings, one of my students called to me and said, "Come here. Here is a man who says the Bible is full of contradictions."

I went over, and it was the same man. The man

evidently thought I would not recognize him, but I did, and I said, "You are the man who lied to me." He dropped his head and said, "Yes."

Another smart, young infidel once said to me, "I don't believe the Bible." I asked him why not.

He replied, "I don't believe that passage where it speaks about Christ calling down fire from heaven to destroy His enemies." When I assured him that there was no such passage in the Bible, he would not believe me.

An infidel in Edinburgh asked me to explain the passage where it said, "Cain went into the land of Nod and took to himself a wife." When I said, "The Bible does not say so," he offered to bet me one hundred pounds that it did.

Colonel Ingersoll, the high priest of the cheaper and more superficial unbelief of the day, is an illustration of this ignorance of the Bible. He said in one of his lectures, "There is not a single kind and loving sentiment attributed to Christ but was uttered by Buddha at least five hundred years before Christ was born."

I would like to know where he finds any utterance of Buddha similar to John 13:34: *A new commandment I give unto you, that ye love one another; as I have loved you, that ye also love one another.* Or John 15:12-13: *This is My commandment, that ye love one another, as I have loved you. Greater love hath no man than this, that a man lay down his life for his friends.* Or Matthew 20:28: *Even as the Son of man came not to be ministered unto, but to minister, and to give His life a ransom for many.*

In another place, Colonel Ingersoll said, "If Christ ever lived on the earth, He was an infidel in His time."

I would like to know what Colonel Ingersoll does with such statements as that of John 10:35: *The Scripture cannot be broken*, or Matthew 5:18: *Till heaven and earth pass, one jot or one tittle shall in no wise pass from the law, till all be fulfilled.* Or Mark 7:13, where speaking of the law of Moses, He calls it the Word of God. Or with Luke 24:27, 44, *And beginning at Moses and all the prophets, he expounded unto them in all the scriptures the things concerning Himself. . . . And he said unto them, These are the words which I spake unto you, while I was yet with you, that all things must be fulfilled which were written in the law of Moses, and in the prophets, and in the Psalms concerning Me.* If this is unbelief, then I am an unbeliever. However, all intelligent people know this is not unbelief, but that Colonel Ingersoll was simply parading his ignorance when he uttered his statement.

One of the leaders of English unbelief some years ago, in an article in one of the secularist journals, spoke of Matthew as a "dispenser of liquors." He knew so little of the Bible that he supposed the word "publican" used of Matthew in the Bible meant publican in the sense of a keeper of a tavern. The man who is probably the most prominent proponent of materialistic unbelief among the Germans is so ignorant of the historic discussions of Christian doctrine that he speaks of the virgin birth of our Lord as "the immaculate conception," and one of the most prominent proponents of unbelief in England does the same thing.

The third cause of unbelief is conceit. Many people tell us that they are unbelievers because they find things in the Bible that they cannot understand, and because there are apparent contradictions in it that they cannot reconcile.

To say that something cannot be true because I cannot understand it, to think that God could utter nothing that would be beyond my understanding, is the ultimate arrogance. It is to assume that I know all things, that I know as much as God knows, and that therefore God could not possibly say anything that I could not understand.

> To say that something cannot be true because I cannot understand it ... is the ultimate arrogance.

To think that no solution to a difficulty can be found because I cannot find the solution is to think that I know all things and that my mind is infinite. It is to think that I am God. Suppose I would take my little child outside around sunset, and say to the child, "Do you see the sun over there?"

"Yes."

"Well, my child, that sun is more than ninety-two million miles away."

Then suppose the child would look up into my face in her mature wisdom of nine years and say, "Father, I know that is not true. The sun is just over there behind the barn." Would this be a revelation of the child's wisdom, or of its ignorance and conceit? The oldest, wisest philosopher compared with the Infinite One is less than a child compared to the wisest of men.

For us to challenge our Father's statements because they seem untrue to us does not reveal us to be philosophers worthy of admiration and applause, but to be foolish children who should be sent to bed. If we find difficulties in the Bible that we cannot explain, a moderate degree of modesty on our part would lead us to say, "If I knew a little more, I might be able to easily explain this difficulty," rather than lead us to say, "This Book that contains a difficulty that I cannot explain surely cannot be from God."

When I was in Birmingham, a man who parades his unbelief by having quotations from various infidels at the head of his notepaper wrote to me and said that the Bible could not be the Word of God because it was full of contradictions. He said that he could send me hundreds of them, but one or two would suffice since they could not be answered. The difficulties he sent were very easy to explain, and I wrote the solution to him. Instead of being shaken in his conviction that the difficulties he held were unsolvable, he wrote that he was sorry that he had chosen such poor examples before, but that now he would send me some more. These were just as easy to explain, but this did not seem to suggest to him that his other apparently unanswerable difficulties would be just as easy to understand as these previously unanswerable difficulties if he only knew a little more.

The fourth cause of unbelief is sin. This is the most common and most fundamental cause of unbelief. Sin causes unbelief in two ways. First, people sin and then give themselves over to unbelief to find comfort in their sin. There is no book that makes people so uneasy in sin as the Bible. Trying to make themselves believe that the Bible is not true gives them some comfort in the pursuit of sin.

People tell you that they have many objections to the Bible, but with the great majority of these people, their greatest objection to the Bible, if they would confess the truth to themselves and to others, is that it condemns their sin and makes them uneasy in their sin.

Second, sin blinds people's eyes to the truth of the Bible and makes it appear as foolishness. There is nothing that blinds the mind to truth like sin. I was once called to deal with an unbeliever. I sat down, and he told me that the reason that he could not be a Christian was because of a difficulty he had with the Bible. I asked him what his difficulty was. He replied that he could not see where Cain got his wife. I said, "Will you come to Christ if I tell you where Cain got his wife?"

There is nothing that blinds the mind to truth like sin.

"Oh," he said, "I will not promise that."

"But," I said, "if that is your difficulty that keeps you from coming to Christ, and if you are an honest man and I remove that difficulty, you will come to Christ."

"No, I will not promise that."

I then went at the root of the matter. I found out that his real difficulty was not about Cain's wife at all, but about another man's wife. It is surprising how often young men who fall into sin and into careless ways of living fall also into unbelief. Through conversation with young men who do not believe the Bible, I have found that there are two specific sins that are the most common cause of unbelief.

My former colleague, Professor W. W. White, was speaking one time in Chicago on the "Mistakes of Ingersoll." At the close of the lecture, a fine-looking man approached him and said, "Professor White, you have no right to say what you have said today. You are a Christian, and I am an unbeliever. I have just as much right to my opinion as you have to yours."

Professor White then asked him a direct question: "Is your life pure?"

The man replied, "That is none of your business. My life is just as pure as yours is."

Then Professor White asked him his name. The man said, "That is none of your business."

"But," said Professor White, "I want to look up your record."

The man declined to give it, and began to back out. However, there were those in the group that gathered around who knew the man's name, and they gave it to Professor White. Within two years from that time, that man was found dead in a Boston hotel, lying beside a young woman who was not his wife, whom he had enticed into unbelief, and who had gone off with him to lecture on unbelief. They were found dead together in this Boston hotel with the gas turned on.

The statement of this fact will make some of you angry, but look into your own hearts and lives and see if there is not some sin at the root of your unbelief. I do not say that all unbelief comes from sin, but after long and careful observation, I do say that a very large part of the current unbelief of the day has sin for its ultimate cause.

The fifth cause of unbelief is resistance to the Holy Spirit. This is a very common cause of unbelief. The Spirit of God moves upon the hearts of men and women, inclining them to accept Christ, but they will not yield to the Spirit of God. They resist the Holy Spirit, the light that He gives to the soul is darkened, and they fall into skepticism or unbelief.

During one of my pastorates, there was a lawyer of excellent abilities who was a most bitter opponent of Christianity. He did what he could to oppose it by bringing atheistic lecturers to town. I looked into this man's previous history. I found that there was a time in the very church of which I was pastor when he was under conviction of sin. He hesitated as to whether he would come out of the world and accept Christ. When pressed upon the subject, he replied, "No, I cannot be a Christian and succeed in my business, and I must support my family."

The light that was dawning upon his soul went out, and darkness and unbelief settled down upon him, exercising such a destructive influence over his life that he lost the confidence of his fellow men. He lost his law practice, and the last I heard, his wife was teaching school to help support the family while he was doing any odd jobs that he could find.

In one of our western colleges, there was a revival

of religion. Two young men in the college set themselves against it. They were determined not to yield. They made an agreement together to meet on a certain evening and go into the chapel and blaspheme the Holy Spirit. They met at the appointed hour, but the heart of one of the young men failed him, and he was later converted. The other man went into the college chapel alone. What he did in there, no one knows, but he came out as white as a sheet. He drifted into unbelief, and he became a leader in one of the secular societies in one of our large cities.

Oh, you men and women who are resisting the Holy Spirit, if we see you five years from now, we will most likely find you atheists, and if we see you ten years from now, in all probability we will find you alcoholics. In the city of Melbourne, more than one person came to me a moral wreck who said that his fall was due to the influence of the noted atheist in that place.

Chapter 10

The Consequences and Cure of Unbelief

In the last chapter, we saw that the causes of unbelief were (1) misrepresentations of Christianity on the part of its professed adherents, (2) ignorance of the Bible, history, and science, (3) conceit, (4) sin, and (5) resistance to the Holy Spirit. Now we will look at the consequences and cure of unbelief.

Consequences of Unbelief

The first consequence of unbelief is sin. Unbelief breeds sin. There is no doubt of that. It is caused by sin, and in turn it brings about offspring that is similar to its ancestors. Sin first entered into human history through questioning God's Word. When the devil tried to lead Eve into disobeying God, he began by throwing out an insinuation that the Word of God was not true.

He first said, *Hath God said* (Genesis 3:1), and then he flatly denied what God said.

The devil was the first lecturer in unbelief. He only had an audience of one, but he reached millions through that lecture. He saw at once the effectiveness of this mode of attack upon us and upon man's moral integrity. From that day to this, the devil has been deceiving people into sin by sowing the seeds of unbelief in their hearts. He well knows what sort of a crop that seed brings forth. When a young man or young woman falls into unbelief, look out for their morals. Unbelief forms a very shaky foundation for an upright character.

A former president of the British National Secular Society, a man well known here in Bolton, who in fact was elected to Parliament from the Bolton district, said, "I have seen the dreadful effects that unbelief produces on people's characters. I have had proof of its deteriorating effects in my own experience. Its tendency is to utter debasement." Occupying the position that he did, Joseph Barker certainly knew unbelief and its consequences, and this testimony of his to its destructive effects upon character is beyond question true.

The second consequence of unbelief is anarchy. Anarchists are necessarily always unbelievers. It is impossible for someone who believes in the Bible to be an anarchist. When the miserable French vagabond and anarchist Vaillant stood upon the gallows, he boasted of his unbelief. His unbelief and his anarchy went hand in hand.

Louis Blanc, one of the great leaders of anarchy, is

reported to have said, "When I was an infant, I rebelled against my nurse. When I was a child, I rebelled against my tutors and my parents. When I was a man, I rebelled against the government. When I die, if there is any heaven and I go there, I will rebel against God."

The acceptance of Christianity would do away with anarchy on the one hand, and it would do away with the oppression of the poor by the rich that leads to anarchy on the other hand.

> The fullness of joy that God intends for us can only come from a living faith in Jesus as the Son of God, and in the Bible as the Word of God.

The third consequence of unbelief is misery and despair. God has created us for fullness of joy, and He has made fullness of joy possible for each one of us. However, the fullness of joy that God intends for us, and which alone can satisfy a soul made in God's image, can only come from a living faith in Jesus as the Son of God, and in the Bible as the Word of God.

Infidels are never completely happy. There may be surface happiness, but it is not, as everyone knows who knows them well, deep and satisfying. One night as I ended a sermon in a New Zealand town, a man somewhat beyond middle life walked in front of the platform as he made his way out of the building. He looked up at me and scowled and said, "I am an unbeliever."

I replied, "You do not need to tell us that; your face shows it. You are one of the most miserable-looking men I have ever seen." I received a letter from him the next day, confessing that he was indeed miserable. Did you ever know a joyous old atheist? As lighthearted as they may seem, at least when they are around groups of people, did you ever see in them that deep, continuous, overflowing joyfulness that is so characteristic of the aged Christian?

On the day of the death of a noted American atheist, I was with a friend of his, and we got to talking about him. He said to me, "Every time of late when I have gone to see him, his wife has said to me, 'Don't tell him that he is growing old. It makes him very angry.'" However, it does not make the aged Christian angry to tell him he is growing old, for he knows he is simply ripening for a better world.

Unbelief and atheism frequently breed despair and suicide. Even the best of pagan writers taught the suitability of suicide. For example, Epictetus says, "The door is open. When you want to, you can leave off playing the game of life." Mrs. Amelia E. Barr, who has made a study of suicide, says, "The advent of Christianity made self-destruction a crime." She further says that the revival of unbelief in France at the time of the Revolution caused the termination of the civil and religious laws against suicide. She still further says, "The great underlying cause of the advance of modern suicide is the advance of lax or skeptical religious views."

Unbelief logically leads to pessimism and despair. Ingersoll himself wrote an editorial in a New York paper in defense of suicide. This editorial was followed in New York and the surrounding neighborhood by a harvest of suicides. The man who wrote the editorial was directly responsible for its consequences, and it is not to be wondered at that the editorial raised a storm of protest and indignation, but his article was the logical outcome of his unbelief.

A poor but brilliant young woman from one of the Southern states came to Chicago at the time of the World's Fair. Her intellectual gifts were so great that she was introduced into the best society, where she spoke about the "new woman." She was led into unbelief by an able advocate of unbelief in Chicago, but her career as an atheist was brief. She soon met a suicide's death in an eastern city, and one branch of the unbelievers of America today meet annually at her grave to commemorate her death. Her brokenhearted father also died by his own hand. Sadly, this is the genuine fruit of unbelief.

If you throw away the Bible, you do not get rid of the gloom, but you do get rid of the light that illumines it.

The fourth consequence of unbelief is a hopeless grave. Colonel Ingersoll once said, "The pulpit has cast a shadow over the cradle and a gloom over the grave." If this is true, it is a most remarkable fact that people, even professedly unbelieving people, are so anxious to have Christian preachers conduct their funerals.

There is a gloom over the grave by nature and by sin, but the Bible dispels the shadow. If you throw away the Bible, you do not get rid of the gloom, but you do get rid of the light that illumines it. Unbelief shrouds the grave in gloom, and the only rays of light are those stolen from Christianity.

Colonel Ingersoll, at his brother's grave, delivered an address that was eloquent in words, but was sad beyond description. As he drew toward the close of that address, he said that hope sees the glimmering of a star through the darkness, but he was not honest enough to say that that star was the Star of Bethlehem.

On the other hand, D. L. Moody, at his brother's grave, sounded forth a note of joy and exultation. Looking into the grave, he quoted 1 Corinthians 15:55-57: *O death, where is thy sting? O grave, where is thy victory? The sting of death is sin; and the strength of sin is the law. But thanks be to God, which giveth us the victory through our Lord Jesus Christ.*

Two men died the same year in America: Colonel Ingersoll, the acknowledged leader of American unbelief, and D. L. Moody, the leader of Christian activity. Compare the deaths and funerals of these two men, and see for yourselves whether the Christian's death or the agnostic's death is the gloomy one.

The death of Colonel Ingersoll was sudden, and without a ray of cheer and brightness, his funeral was unutterably dismal. His wife and daughter, who loved him, could not bear to have the body taken from the house until the beginning of decay made it an absolute necessity. It was all they had, and they despairingly clung to that decaying body. The scene at the crematory, as described in the daily papers, was enough to make the heart of anyone ache, no matter how little one might be in sympathy with the views of the unfortunate man who had passed into eternity.

On the other hand, the death and funeral of Mr.

Moody were triumphant in every detail. Early on the morning of his departure from this world, his oldest son was sitting beside his bed. He heard his father speaking in a low tone of voice, and he leaned over to listen. These were the words that he heard: "Earth is receding. Heaven is opening. God is calling."

"You are dreaming, Father," said the son.

"No, Will, this is no dream. I have been within the gates. I have seen the children's faces."

The family was summoned. Mr. Moody rallied. A while later, he began to sink again, and he was heard to say, "Is this death? This is not bad. There is no valley. This is bliss. This is glorious."

"Father," said his daughter, "you must not leave us. We cannot spare you."

The dying man replied, "I am not going to throw my life away. If God has any more work for me to do, I will get well and do it; but if God is calling, I must up and off."

He rallied again. He gained sufficient strength to arise from the bed and walk over to the window. He sat down in a chair and talked with his family. He began to think he would recover, and was contemplating sending for his pastor to pray for his recovery. Then, beginning to sink again, he asked them to help him back to the bed. As he was sinking, his daughter knelt by the bed and began to pray for his recovery, but he said, "No, no, Emma, don't pray that. God is calling. This is my coronation day. I have been long looking forward to it," and the heroic warrior was swept up into the presence of the King.

At the funeral, all was triumphant. His son said to me before the service, "Remember, there is to be nothing of sadness in the service. We want nothing but triumph here today." The body was carried to the church by students from one of the schools that he had founded. It lay in an open casket in front of the pulpit. Right in front of it, with unveiled faces, sat his wife and daughter and sons listening with peaceful faces to the words that were spoken, and joining in the hymns of gladness and praise and victory. When others had ceased speaking, the oldest son arose and gladly gave a testimony for his father and the power of his faith.

Is it Christianity that throws a gloom over the grave? Is the Christian's grave the gloomy one and the unbeliever's the bright one? Who ever heard of a Christian repenting on his deathbed that he had been a Christian? It is not at all uncommon, though, for unbelievers to repent on their deathbed that they had been unbelievers.

The fifth consequence of unbelief is eternal ruin. We are told in Mark 16:16, *He that believeth and is baptized shall be saved, but he that believeth not shall be condemned.* We are told in John 3:36, *He that believeth in the Son hath everlasting life, but he that believeth not the Son shall not see life, but the wrath of God abideth on him.*

We have all sinned, and the only way to find forgiveness is by the acceptance of the Sin-bearer whom God has provided. If we prefer to be unbelievers and reject Him, we have no hope. Jesus is the only Savior who has ever proved capable of saving people from the power of sin here, so we can rest assured that He is the only One who will prove capable of saving people from the consequences of sin hereafter.

However, there are many people who do not claim to be unbelievers, who are not theoretically so, but are practically so. All who reject Christ are really unbelievers, and they will be lost. As Ethan Allen, a brave soldier but hopeless atheist, stood at his daughter's deathbed, she turned to him

> **All who reject Christ are really unbelievers, and they will be lost.**

and asked whether she should accept his unbelief or her mother's faith, and the humbled man advised her to accept her mother's faith in that difficult hour.

The Cure for Unbelief

The great cure for unbelief is Christian living on the part of professed Christians. There is no argument for Christianity like a Christlike life. Many skeptics and unbelievers have been won by the life of someone who did not merely intellectually believe in Christ, but who lived like Him in his daily walk.

As Robert McAll lay dead in his coffin in Paris, a workman of Paris, a former anarchist, stood by his coffin weeping. The crying man was asked, "Are you a relative?"

"No."

"Why, then, do you weep?"

"He saved me."

"What did he say?"

"He said nothing," replied the former anarchist. "It was his face." The Christlike character shining out in a Christlike countenance had saved this man.

I was once asked to call upon a woman of brilliant gifts who was an unbeliever. She said, "There is one thing I cannot get around, and that is my father's life." Not long after, by the power of the truth as exemplified in her father's life, leading her to a deeper study of the Bible, she came out as an openly professed follower of Jesus Christ.

In the second place, the cure for unbelief is a surrendered will on the part of the unbeliever. Jesus says, *Whosoever willeth to do His will, he shall know of the teaching, whether it be of God or whether I speak from Myself* (John 7:17). Anyone afflicted with the malady of skepticism can find a remedy if he follows this simple direction.

Nothing clarifies the spiritual vision as much as a surrendered will.

Nothing clarifies the spiritual vision as much as a surrendered will. By the simple act of the surrender of the will to God, many people have found the haze of unbelief scatter in a moment. When I was in New Zealand, a well-known and well-educated commercial traveler came to me and said, "My friends want me to speak to you. I am an agnostic, but I know that you cannot help me."

I told him that I thought that I could, but he was sure that I could not. "What do you believe?" I asked.

"I don't know as I believe anything."

"Do you not believe that there is an absolute difference between right and wrong?"

"Yes, I do."

"Will you take your stand upon the right to follow it wherever it carries you?"

"I think I am doing that now."

"Will you definitely here today take your stand upon the right to follow it wherever it carries you, no matter what it costs?"

He said, "I will."

"Do you know that God does not answer prayer?"

"No, I do not know that God does not answer prayer."

"Well, here is a possible clue to knowledge. Will you follow it? Will you pray this prayer: "Oh God, if there is any God, show me if Jesus Christ is Your Son, and if you show me that He is, I promise to accept Him as my Savior and confess Him before the world"?

"Yes," he said. "I will do that, but it won't do any good."

"John tells us in John 20:31, *These are written, that ye might believe that Jesus is the Christ, the Son of God; and that believing ye might have life through His name.* Will you take the Gospel of John and read it? Read carefully, slowly, and thoughtfully. Do not try to believe it and do not try to disbelieve it, but simply be willing to be convinced of the truth. Before you read, kneel down and ask God to show you what truth there may be in the verses you are about to read, and promise Him that whatever He shows you to be true, you will take your stand upon."

He agreed to do this also. He then left, assuring me that nothing would come of it. Some weeks later, in Dunedin, this man's wife came to me and said, "I have had a letter from my husband that I do not understand. He said I could show it to you." In the letter, he said that he thought he was converted, but he was not quite sure yet. He wrote that she could show this letter to me and to the minister, but not to anyone else until he was perfectly sure of his position. He afterward came out fully as a believer in the Bible and in Christ.

The third part of the cure for unbelief is the study of the Word of God. People do not need to study books about the evidence for Christianity, for the Bible is its own best proof. Let anyone who honestly seeks the truth, anyone who sincerely desires to know the truth and is willing to obey it whatever it costs, earnestly study the Bible, and he will soon become convinced that it is the Word of God.

In my first pastorate, there was a member of my church who had a brother who lectured on scientific subjects, but was an unbeliever. Sometimes he would lecture on the contradictions between science and the Bible. The member of the church came to me and asked if I would pray for her brother that he would be converted. I agreed to do so. A while later, she came to me and said that her brother had written her a letter and said that he had become a Christian. In this letter he gave her the reason for his conversion: "I have been recently studying the Bible, and have become convinced that it is the Word of God." It would have been good if he had studied the Bible before he lectured about it and the alleged contradictions between it and science.

In another one of my pastorates, I had a friend who lived across the street from me who was an agnostic. Though he was an agnostic and I was a Christian minister, we were good friends, for I believe that a Christian and a Christian minister should get to know all classes of people. I do not believe at all in the division of society into men, women, and ministers. I think a minister should be a man among men. How can we expect to influence men unless we rub elbows with them?

Our Master was not too good to associate with all kinds and conditions of people, even the most depraved and outcast. Are we better than our Master? I read in my Bible that Christians are the salt of the earth. How on earth can we expect the salt to exert its preservative influence upon the meat if we put all the salt in one barrel and the meat in another?

This man and I were good friends. We often met and talked together. One night we were standing together on his front lawn as the sun was going down, when he suddenly said, "Mr. Torrey, I am sixty-six years of age. I cannot live many more years. I have no one to leave my money to, and I cannot take it with me. I would give every penny of it if I could believe as you do."

I replied, "That is very easy. I can tell you how." We went into the house, and I asked his wife for a sheet of paper. I wrote upon it the following words: "I believe that there is an absolute difference between right and wrong (I did not say I believe that there is a God, for this man was an agnostic, neither affirming nor denying the existence of God, and you have to begin where a man is), and I hereby take my stand upon the right to follow it wherever it carries me. I promise to make an honest search to find if Jesus Christ is the Son of God, and if I find that He is, I promise to accept Him as my Savior and confess Him as such before the world."

Having written this out, I handed it to my friend and asked, "Will you sign that?"

He replied, "Why, anybody should be willing to sign that. You only ask me to agree to do what my own conscience tells me I should do. Anybody should be willing to sign that."

"Will you sign it?" I asked.

He replied more earnestly, "Anybody should be willing to sign that."

I said, "Will *you* sign it?"

Still more earnestly, he said, "Anybody should be willing to sign that."

"Will you sign it?"

"I will think about it," he said.

He never signed it. He died as he had lived – without God, without Christ, and without hope. He went out into the darkness of a Christless eternity. He told the truth about one thing. He did not take one penny of his money with him. They laid him in a Christless grave. He is now in a Christless eternity, but whose fault was it? A way was shown him out of darkness and into light – a way that he admitted his own conscience told him he should take – and he would not take it.

The same way has been shown to you. Follow it, and it will lead you as it has led thousands of others.

It will lead you out of the uncertainty and the restless-ness and the ultimate despair of unbelief, and into the certitude, the joy, the victory, and the ultimate glory of an intelligent faith in the Bible as the Word of God, and in Jesus Christ as the Son of God.

Reuben A. Torrey
– A Brief Biography

Reuben A. Torrey was an author, conference speaker, pastor, evangelist, Bible college dean, and more. Torrey was born in Hoboken, New Jersey, on January 28, 1856. He graduated from Yale University in 1875 and from Yale Divinity School in 1878, when he became the pastor of a Congregational church in Garrettsville, Ohio. Torrey married Clara Smith in 1879, with whom he had five children.

In 1882, he went to Germany, where he studied at the universities at Leipzig and Erlangen. Upon returning to the United States, Torrey pastored in Minneapolis, and was also in charge of the Congregational City Mission Society. In 1889, Dwight L. Moody called upon Torrey to lead his Chicago Evangelization Society, which later became the Moody Bible Institute. Beginning in 1894, Torrey was also the pastor of the Chicago Avenue Church, which was later called the Moody Memorial

Church. He was a chaplain with the YMCA during the Spanish-American War, and was also a chaplain during World War I.

Torrey traveled all over the world leading evangelistic tours, preaching to the unsaved. It is believed that more than one hundred thousand were saved under his preaching. In 1908, he helped start the Montrose Bible Conference in Pennsylvania, which continues today. He became dean of the Bible Institute of Los Angeles (now Biola University) in 1912, and was the pastor of the Church of the Open Door in Los Angeles from 1915 to 1924.

Torrey continued speaking all over the world and holding Bible conferences. He died in Asheville, North Carolina, on October 26, 1928.

Torrey was a very active evangelist and soul winner, speaking to people everywhere he went, in public and in private, about their souls, seeking to lead the lost to Jesus. He authored more than forty books, including *How to Bring Men to Christ, How to Pray, How to Study the Bible for Greatest Profit, How to Obtain Fullness of Power in Christian Life and Service,* and *Why God Used D. L. Moody,* and also helped edit the twelve-volume book about the fundamentals of the faith, titled *The Fundamentals.* He was also known as a man of prayer, and his teaching, preaching, writing, and his entire life proved that he walked closely with God.

Other Similar Titles

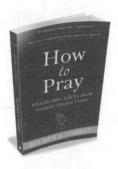

How to Pray, by Reuben A. Torrey

It is not necessary that the whole church prays to begin with. Great revivals always begin first in the hearts of a few men and women whom God arouses by His Spirit to believe in Him as a living God, as a God who answers prayer, and upon whose heart He lays a burden from which no rest can be found except in persistent crying unto God.

May God use this book to inspire many who are currently prayerless, or nearly so, to pray earnestly. May God stir up your own heart to be one of those burdened to pray, and to pray until God answers.

Available where books are sold.

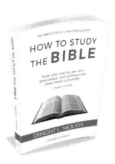

How to Study the Bible, by Dwight L. Moody

There is no situation in life for which you cannot find some word of consolation in Scripture. If you are in affliction, if you are in adversity and trial, there is a promise for you. In joy and sorrow, in health and in sickness, in poverty and in riches, in every condition of life, God has a promise stored up in His Word for you.

This classic book by Dwight L. Moody brings to light the necessity of studying the Scriptures, presents methods which help stimulate excitement for the Scriptures, and offers tools to help you comprehend the difficult passages in the Scriptures. To live a victorious Christian life, you must read and understand what God is saying to you. Moody is a master of using stories to illustrate what he is saying, and you will be both inspired and convicted to pursue truth from the pages of God's Word.

Available where books are sold.

The Pursuit of God, by A. W. Tozer

To have found God and still to pursue Him is a paradox of love, scorned indeed by the too-easily-satisfied religious person, but justified in happy experience by the children of the burning heart. Saint Bernard of Clairvaux stated this holy paradox in a musical four-line poem that will be instantly understood by every worshipping soul:

> *We taste Thee, O Thou Living Bread,*
> *And long to feast upon Thee still:*
> *We drink of Thee, the Fountainhead*
> *And thirst our souls from Thee to fill.*

Come near to the holy men and women of the past and you will soon feel the heat of their desire after God. Let A. W. Tozer's pursuit of God spur you also into a genuine hunger and thirst to truly know God.

Available where books are sold.